Improve Your Handwriting

Teach Yourself®

Improve Your Handwriting

Rosemary Sassoon
and Gunnlaugur SE Briem

For UK order enquiries: please contact Bookpoint Ltd, 130 Milton Park, Abingdon, Oxon OX14 4SB. Telephone: +44 (0) 1235 827720. Fax: +44 (0) 1235 400454. Lines are open 09.00–17.00, Monday to Saturday, with a 24-hour message answering service. Details about our titles and how to order are available at www.teachyourself.co.uk

For USA order enquiries: please contact McGraw-Hill Customer Services, PO Box 545, Blacklick, OH 43004-0545, USA. Telephone: 1-800-722-4726. Fax: 1-614-755-5645.

For Canada order enquiries: please contact McGraw-Hill Ryerson Ltd, 300 Water St, Whitby, Ontario L1N 9B6, Canada. Telephone: 905 430 5000. Fax: 905 430 5020.

British Library Cataloguing in Publication Data: a catalogue record for this title is available from the British Library.

Library of Congress Catalog Card Number: on file.

First published in UK 1984 by Hodder Education, part of Hachette UK.

First published in US 1984 by The McGraw-Hill Companies, Inc.

This edition published 2014.

ISBN 978 1444 1 0379 3

eISBN 978 1 444 1 3110 9

Typeset by Cenveo® Publisher Services.

Printed and bound by CPI Group (UK) Ltd, Croydon, CR0 4YY for John Murray Learning, an Hachette UK Company, 338 Euston Road, London NW1 3BH.

Impression number 16

Year 2018

Contents

Meet the authors

Rosemary Sassoon specializes in the educational and medical aspects of handwriting. Her background is in lettering and design but it is her fieldwork and research into adult problems that led to this book. She lectures widely and is the author of many books, including *Handwriting: The Way to Teach It*, *Handwriting Problems in the Secondary School* and *Handwriting of the Twentieth Century*. She was awarded a PhD by the University of Reading for her work on the effects of different models and teaching methods on how children learn to write. She is the designer of the Sassoon family of typefaces meant for educational purposes and maximum legibility.

Gunnlaugur SE Briem is a designer and lives in California. His postgraduate studies in Copenhagen, Basel and London culminated with a PhD from the Royal College of Art. He took part in the introduction of italic handwriting in his native Iceland, where his method and teaching aids have been tested in classrooms for over 20 years. Some examples are on his website www.briem.net. He is on the advisory board of *Visible Language*, the research journal. He also publishes free e-books on letterforms and related subjects at http://operina.com

Introduction

In this age of the computer some people seem to believe that handwriting is redundant. In some parts of the world they have even stopped teaching it as a subject. However, to make your mark is a basic human need. Will people ever stop wanting to express themselves in handwritten script? If it stops being taught in some schools, then we may end up with a two-tiered society – those who can only communicate through various technological means, and those who can also write.

Handwriting is not just for communication. It is far more. It is how you present yourself to the world, and, rightly or wrongly, it is often how the world judges you. It is so unfair. All too often people have not been adequately taught how to write from the start, then later they themselves are blamed for their poor writing.

Writing by hand is still a vital skill worldwide. Even in countries where computers are in constant use, taking many of the tedious tasks off tired hands, they cannot do everything. For instance, it may be many years before they are universally approved for use in examinations. What about the vital task of taking notes of all kinds? Today, most of us need flexible ways of writing starting with a fast, almost scribble for jobs that only we need to decipher. Then we need a progressively slower, more legible hand for other purposes. Some of us may need a good kind of show handwriting, not forgetting those who yearn for a truly beautiful script.

Then there are times when a typed letter is inappropriate and you want something more personal. You want something special. We all know the feeling when an envelope arrives and you recognize the hand of a much-loved friend or relative. There are so many reasons for keeping up handwriting and acquiring a satisfactory personal script. What is more, unfair though it is, we are often judged by the appearance of our handwriting by the outside world. Just addressing that envelope may be revealing.

Writing by hand can make a difference to what you write as well. It is interesting to learn that the more creative writers and poets are, the more likely they are to prefer writing by hand. It is that feeling of straight from the mind to the paper via the hand.

What is happening around the world? People in many countries use a different script and, in increasing numbers, want to learn our alphabet. This book will be just as relevant and useful to them.

It is a good idea to explain what handwriting is in relation to the individual. It is a trace of a trained movement of the hand when that hand holds a pen and the pen is in contact with the paper. Handwriting movement is a habit that is very strong and individual; it is a mixture of what you are taught and your personality. In handwriting, individual likes and dislikes are also strong. Views on style vary considerably. Some people admire italic handwriting while others prefer a rounder, more upright script. Some people cling closely to the model that they learned at school, while others have developed a fast practical script to suit their own needs. If their own way works for them, they may find it hard to appreciate another style.

We want people with any style of handwriting to be able to relate to this book and learn from it. Many manuals stress the importance of a particular style and imply that their own model is all-important. It is supposed to be followed closely so, whoever they are, everyone is meant to produce a replica of the author's writing. Maybe this worked in the past, but today we should think differently.

One of the advantages of having two authors is that, although we are both designers and letterers, we have very different handwriting. Briem's is italic and very beautiful. Mine is fast, practical and not very beautiful. Now it is even less beautiful as I have had a stroke. I know only too well the problems of having a hand that will not obey me, and not being able to write as I might wish. Serious problems like this are also dealt with in this book. We have tried to explain how to deal with the most usual ones while understanding that some can be solved and others only alleviated.

Our model is not meant to be slavishly copied or followed forever. We understand that, if you altered your handwriting completely, you might not feel it represented the real you any more. Our model is meant to train in a basic movement and an economical shape. Then you can adapt this to your own personal slant and width of letter using whatever pen suits you best. We have provided several samples of how this has worked for different people.

There is a more formal alphabet later on in the book if that is what you are looking for. In most cases, however, it will be a matter of building on what you already have rather than altering everything about your handwriting. We would suggest that your writing habits should only radically alter if they cause you actual pain or stop you from achieving your aim.

This is not the attitude to take when teaching children. They need informed teaching and a structured but flexible method to ensure that they have the necessary training from the start. This ensures that they can develop the good writing habits that can last them a lifetime. You might be suffering now from just that lack of training.

Do not worry that we are trying to alter your character or take over a part of you. By the time you have diagnosed your particular problems and used our exercises to tackle them, your handwriting may have altered considerably. However, it will still be your handwriting, not ours.

Rosemary Sassoon

We thought it would be interesting, and only fair, to start with examples of our own handwriting:

To me letterforms are full of excitement and wonder. When I went to school in Iceland I was taught a debased copperplate and got awful marks for penmanship. I came across italic handwriting in my late teens and it changed my life.

Gunnlaugur SE Briem

As a calligrapher I *can* write an italic hand, but my everyday writing is quite different. It is extremely fast and not very beautiful. Sometimes it is barely legible, but it is practical and lets me fit a lot of writing into a busy life.
I know all the rules and break most of them

Rosemary Sassoon

How to use this book

You can think of this book as a repair manual for handwriting. To make it easy for you to find out exactly what needs to be changed there are two full chapters of questions and answers in Part one (Chapters 1 and 2). They deal with most of the things that can and do go wrong with handwriting, but only you can tell which apply to you. When you have diagnosed your own trouble, you can turn to Part two in the book, which deals with the cure. However, it is worth reading through the whole book even when you know that you have spotted your own particular fault. Learning about writing – how it works and where it goes wrong – is an interesting study in itself.

What this book can do for you

First of all you must learn to be self-critical. If you want to improve your handwriting, you need to see where it has gone wrong. When you have learned how to diagnose your particular problems, you are well on the way to solving them.

You will need the best conditions if you are to make good progress in retraining. There is no reason to make your life more difficult, so try to get rid of the handicaps from the start. You are more comfortable and write better if your table is the correct height. It *does* matter where you place your paper and how you hold your pen. Maybe you do not think that you need to be told simple things like this, but please keep an open mind until you have read the reasons why. If you are left-handed, you will be glad to know that there is a special section for you (Chapter 4). Everybody is encouraged to experiment with pens and paper to find what works best.

Chapter 5 on more serious problems explains that some difficulties are cosmetic, some are educational, and some could be classified as medical. This chapter can only skim over the surface of the more serious implications of handwriting problems. It tries, however, to help the increasing number of people who may have given up hope of ever being able to write adequately again because of an accident or illness. The need for this chapter has been highlighted by the many letters from those who read previous editions of this book.

In Part two, Chapter 6, the first exercises are very simple. They show you how to relax. The next set in Chapter 7 teaches you control and regularity, and it is meant to train your hand and eye to work together. The exercises are really necessary. Please do not leave them out.

The model in Part two, Chapter 8 is a special training alphabet to sort out your letter construction and movement: it is *not* the way you are supposed to write in the end. It will make you more analytical about letters. Next you learn simple joins in Chapter 9 – if you need to – then faster and more personal ligatures in Chapter 10. They will help you to develop a mature cursive hand.

The 'before and after' examples in Part three are all genuine cases. Go through them carefully – they may hold the answer to your problems. In Part four, Chapter 12 on layout has been given more prominence in this edition. As more and more people rely on computers to do everything for them they become less aware of the simple rules that make a page of writing better in appearance and easier to read. The chapter on layout is followed by a more formal model in Chapter 13.

When it comes to style, you must make your choice. You will learn how to modify and personalize the training alphabet. Everybody's handwriting is different and of course your own is influenced by your character. This book will give you a greater insight into writing. You will end up taking much more notice of other people's hands too – both good and bad.

What you must do for yourself

It will not be enough to read through this book and just do a few exercises on the way. It may take quite a lot of work and willpower to change whatever is worrying you about your handwriting. The determination to improve must come from you.

If you have been unhappy about your writing, you may have stopped using it. It may even be a visible reminder of failure. Handwriting is meant to be used, so remember that real practice is needed. Try keeping a diary; it is a good way of making sure that you write something every day. On the other hand, you may already need to write a lot and just want to speed up your handwriting or improve its appearance. You will have the motivation and the opportunity to exercise and practise.

Sometimes your handwriting is not entirely to blame. Poor spelling and grammar can cause hesitation and lack of confidence. All this shows up only too easily in written work. It is a good idea to sort out the problems one by one. Spelling often improves as you become a more relaxed writer. Our repetitive letter patterns separate the spelling element from skill training. Get your handwriting to flow and you relieve one urgent worry. Then you can tackle the other problems.

Another hint: you can take the tension out of writing important letters by making several rough drafts. First plan the wording and correct the spelling and grammar. Then you are free to concentrate on an attractive layout and good handwriting.

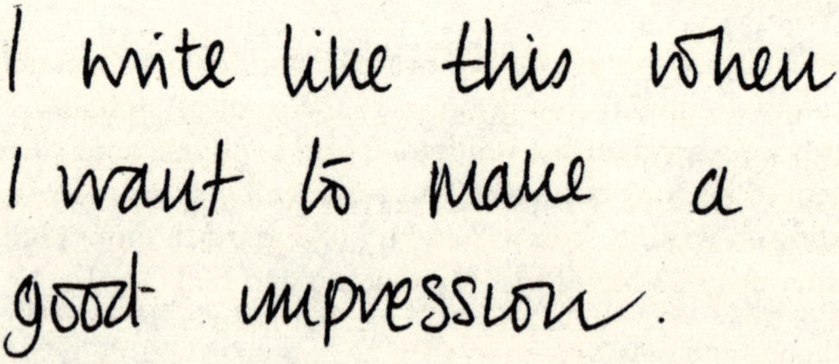

This is Nancy's careful handwriting. She uses it for special occasions ...

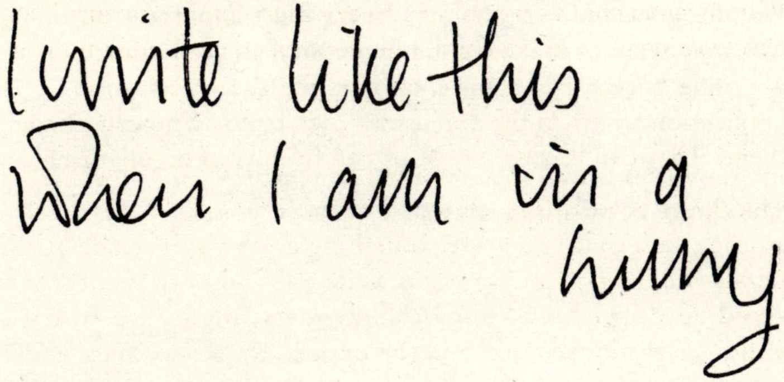

... this is her quick personal scribble.
Like most people she has at least two levels of writing.

This book can help you improve some aspects of your handwriting, but cannot change you altogether. If your life is rushed and hectic, it will show in your writing. If you take great pride in your attention to detail, it may be harder for you to relax your standards and speed things up. Your life is your own and some problems you will have to deal with yourself.

Wanting to change your handwriting may be an indication that you are ready, or wanting, to change a whole lot of other things in your life as well. You alone can decide what you wish to change and why.

Sorting out your priorities

You should think of your handwriting as a tool that you use in your job and everyday life. Then you can consider your personal priorities. This is important in deciding what you want to change.

Maybe speed is your top priority. Students in particular need a fast hand, and never more so than at examination time. Anyone who has to take notes depends on getting things down fast.

But perhaps a clear legible hand is more important to you. If someone else has to read back what you have written, then legibility is really important.

Equally, good presentation may be the most important factor. You may want to make a good impression so need as mature a writing as possible. Some employers prefer to receive job application letters in the applicant's own hand. Who can blame them? They can learn a lot about you from your handwriting.

The choice of priorities, therefore, must be yours.

Part one

Handwriting problems

What is good handwriting?

As far as I can tell
to teach children to write
from 'script' letters at the

Good handwriting is above all legible.

I hope all is well with you. Please
pass along my thanks to our hosts!

Then it is flowing, it is consistent and has a distinct character.

enormous pleasure and I do thank
you most gratefully. This kind of

Handwriting is an expression of individuality.

You might even persuade
him to come along to the
next course!

Different people have different handwriting.

1

Self-diagnosis

How to begin diagnosing your writing problems

Some faults can be detected just by looking at a finished piece of writing. So take an example of something you have already written. Do not write or select anything specially for this purpose. Just pick up an old letter, some notes, or even a shopping list – something quite ordinary. Ask yourself these questions:

1 Are the basic letters constructed properly, or are they poorly shaped, making the writing difficult to read?

2 Do the letters join up and flow?

3 Are the strokes leaning in all directions?

4 Is the writing consistent?

5 Is it mature enough?

6 Is it too complicated or fussy?

7 Is it too large or too small?

8 Is the writing itself quite good but the layout and spacing unsatisfactory?

Now for the diagnosis and where to find the cure:

1 If your individual letters are not properly formed, your writing may be difficult to read. Perhaps your **a**'s and **g**'s are left open so they can be confused with **u** or **y**. Maybe you do not finish one letter before starting the next so an **n** looks like an **r**, or an **a** like an **o**.

'The phone rang'. This writing is bad. The **a** is so misshapen that you are likely to misread the word. Most of the letters are badly formed.

Perhaps there is no difference between your arched letters so that **u** and **n** can get muddled up.

Chapter 8 provides a model that you can use to retrain the shape of your letters. We explain there how and why it works. Choose the family or families of letters that you need most.

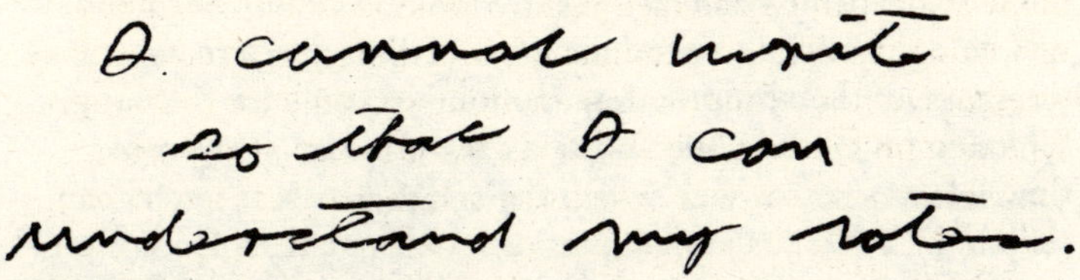

'I cannot write so that I can understand my notes.' These letters are so poorly formed that it is not surprising that the writer can hardly read his own notes.

Maybe you start your letters at the wrong point or you make your strokes in the wrong direction, with the result that you find problems when joining up your writing. You might have a personal shorthand that no one else can read because your joined-up letters form unrecognizable symbols. Instead of oo you might be getting ɑɒ. You could be losing a stroke for the same reason. n and m lead to ir and hir instead of in and him. These problems are more difficult to cure, as you will have to retrain your writing movement. First of all, study the analysis of the individual letters on pages 79–104. The point of entry and direction of each stroke is shown. Read Chapter 8 carefully. Remember to use stroke-related groups of letters when you start practising. Then you are repeating, comparing and improving similar shapes and thoroughly training in the correct movement.

The rounded v in 'receiving' reads clearly. The same shape representing 'ir' in 'shirt' is confusing. 'Time' reads as 'tine'.

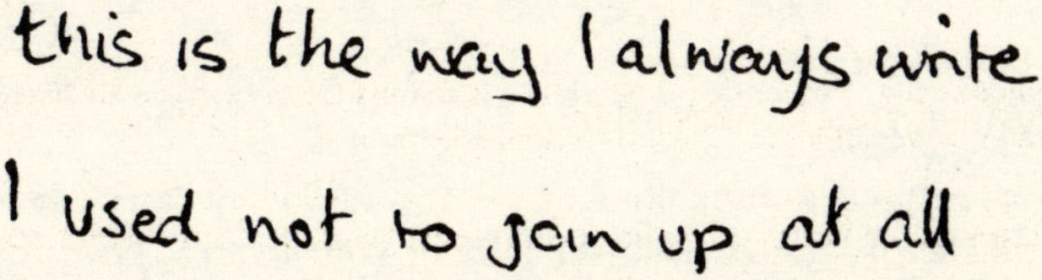

This girl wanted to join up but found if difficult to change from straight letters to a flowing movement.

2 If the letters do not join up and you want to develop a more cursive (joined) writing, then you might have to exercise quite hard to change your writing movement. The neater you print, the more difficult you may find it. This is because your hand will be accustomed to producing the pressure pattern as well as the shape of the abrupt letters. To join up you have to change direction on the baseline and relax the pressure at the same time. However, it is well worth the effort. Separate letters can seldom be as fast as joined ones or look as mature. Do not go to the other extreme. Too many joins are as bad as too few. The way we hold our pens and rest our hand on the table to write means that we need penlifts every few letters.

When you follow up with the personal modification exercises in Chapter 10, you may find that the angle of your handwriting has changed. As you relax and speed up, you may develop a more forward slant.

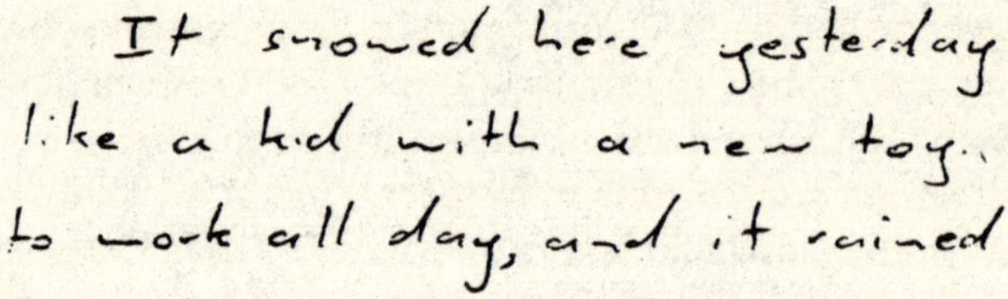

The Australian who wrote this went back to a quick print because he could not speed up the complicated cursive that he had been taught at school.

3 If the letters are leaning in all directions, there can be several reasons:

- Maybe you have trouble in controlling your pen and keeping lines parallel.
- Maybe you were taught a mixture of styles and you have ended up using a bit of each.
- Maybe you are over-tense. This can affect your writing, pushing your strokes aslant.
- Maybe your joining strokes are at fault. They can come up at different angles from the base of your letters. Then they affect the next upright stroke. This also happens when you do not finish off one letter properly before starting the next.

All these faults will make your writing increasingly hard to read as you speed it up.

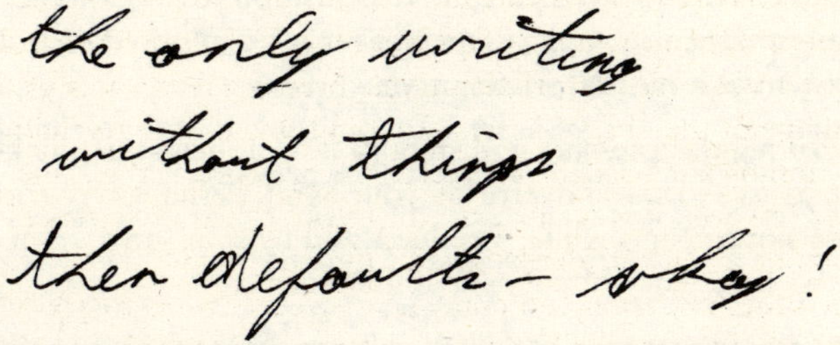

These letters are falling about in all directions. The effect is disturbing and difficult to read.

This is the only time that we suggest using the exercises as a complete course. Work through the book from Chapter 3 to Chapter 10.

The relaxing exercises on page 28 will help with any tension. You may not need the control exercises (pages 58–60), but they certainly will not do you any harm.

4 If your writing is not consistent, first make sure that you are giving yourself the best possible writing conditions. Is the writing the same at the top of the page as at the bottom? Are your letter shapes the same even from one line to the next? If not, read Chapter 3 on practical matters. Pay special attention to what you write with and what you write on. Your posture is important, and where you place your paper too. Chapter 7 on rhythm and texture will also be useful.

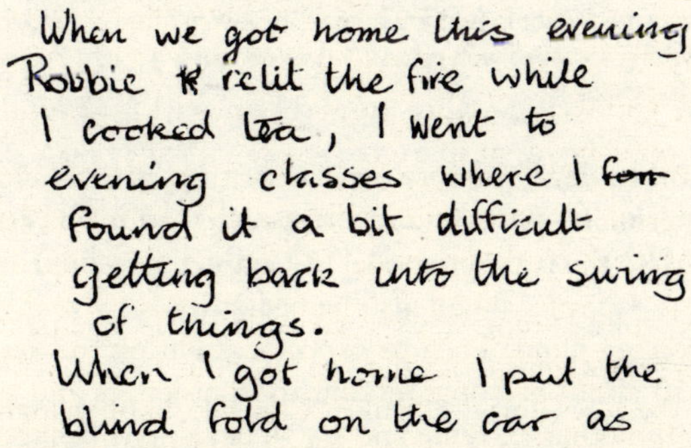

In this writing both the joining and the slant are inconsistent.

Maybe you have been taught a style that does not suit you. The model in Chapter 8 will help you to understand more about letters. You will be in a better position to judge what sort of writing you want. Remember that no imposed style is as consistent as a natural writing style.

Aim for regular pressure and smooth flow. If necessary, make more pauses to avoid overtiring your hand. Perhaps try writing a little slower for a while. Tiredness and tension show up in your writing. They often make it uneven.

If you are at a stage in life when you are changing and developing, this will be reflected in your handwriting. It will be variable too until you settle down.

5 If it is not mature enough, you may feel that your writing does not present you to others as you would like it to – or even as you are.

Writing can look immature for a number of reasons. Some people remain too long on, or keep too close to, a taught model. Unjoined writing can also look childish. Sometimes large writing can give the same impression.

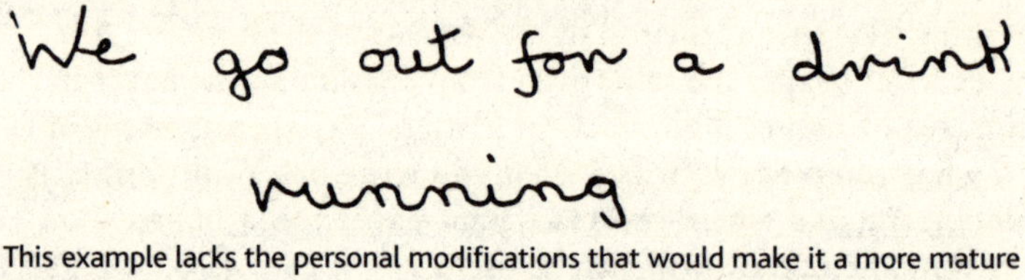

This example lacks the personal modifications that would make it a more mature script. Some people find it hard to develop a personal hand. They stick closely to what they were taught in primary school. They were often praised for their neat handwriting and even won prizes for it. Their writiing might be neat but it remains rather childish.

If you want to develop more mature writing, first try changing pens. Experiment with all kinds to see what suits you best (see page 29). Use the training model in Chapter 8 to improve your letterforms. Chapter 9 will also be necessary for you if you need a more flowing hand. Then pay special attention to Chapter 10, which is all about personal modification of letters and joins. Do not go to the other extreme and try to develop too elaborate a writing. This will not look mature at all, only fussy and affected. Stop worrying about your writing. Practise, and you should become consistent in a natural style that reflects your personality.

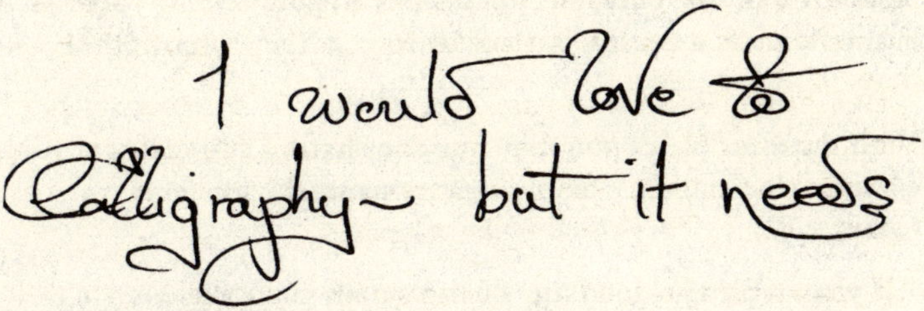

This would be rather too intricate for most people.

6 If it is too complicated, simplifying your style will gain you speed and legibility. You may have developed unnecessary flourishes or twirls in your writing. They can be difficult to discard, but it is worth trying. They can slow you down and make your writing difficult to read. To other people they often look foolish.

At school you may have been taught a looped cursive that is based on copperplate. The letters are all meant to join up, so your hand cannot be moved along during a long word. At speed, the loops often deteriorate into a tangled mess. By the end of a long word you cannot read a thing.

You should be able to go straight to the model in Chapter 8 to find a more economical way of writing. Your writing probably flows already, so you will not need to spend much time learning formal joins. Study Chapter 10 to help develop a more personal hand. Then you should be able to see how much you have gained in speed and legibility by simplifying your writing.

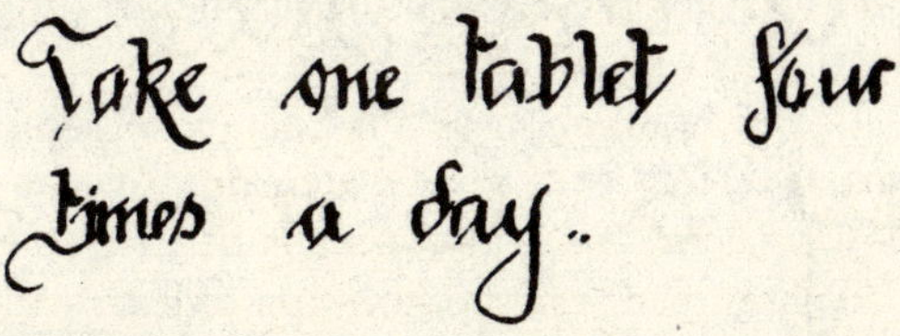

This is more lettering than handwriting. Unless it comes naturally, it can look too fussy.

There are other kinds of complicated hands. Sometimes a distorted italic writing has left you with exaggerated exit or entry strokes. Or you may have tried to copy someone else's handwriting. The characteristics that you admire may come naturally to that person but not to you, so they interrupt the flow of your writing.

With these problems you may find the rhythm and texture exercises in Chapter 7 helpful before using the model in Chapter 8.

7 **If your writing is too large or too small,** you must ask yourself why this is happening.

A large handwriting can be confident and striking; or it can exaggerate any fault. Long lines can become wavery, and make the writing weak. Very large writing can look immature or pompous. The size depends on whom you are writing to and what you are writing about. It is also wasteful of time and materials.

Small handwriting can be an indication of tension. It can also mean that the writer is very tidy or economically minded. However, small writing is often difficult to read. You need to be careful that it is legible. Therefore you may have to go too slowly.

If you want to change the size of your writing to make it either smaller or larger, the first thing to do is to change your pen.

To reduce the size of your writing, use a nib or fibre tip with a finer point. Exercise on paper with closely spaced lines. The distance between the lines will help you to control the size of your letters.

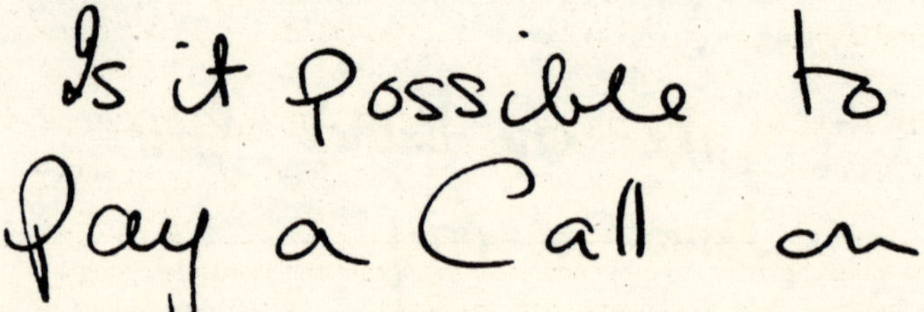

This is a large, clear hand, but extravagant.

To enlarge handwriting that is too small, first try some of the relaxing scribbles on page 28. Make them bold. Then you might try some lines that are spaced far enough apart to encourage larger writing. You may find suitably lined paper or you may have to rule some yourself. Then you might find it helpful to try out different types of pens, preferably those with fatter points.

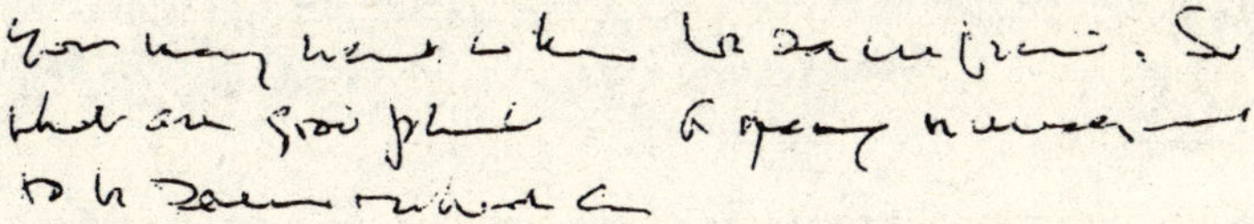

Small writing must be carefully constructed or it is hard to read.

8 If your writing is good but the way it is set out on the page is unsatisfactory, turn to Chapter 12, which deals with layout and presentation. If you find it difficult to keep your writing in straight lines, turn to pages 31–3 where lines are discussed.

This chapter has dealt with the problems you find by looking at something you have already written. The next one is also about recognizing problems. It is different because you have to ask yourself questions about the act of writing.

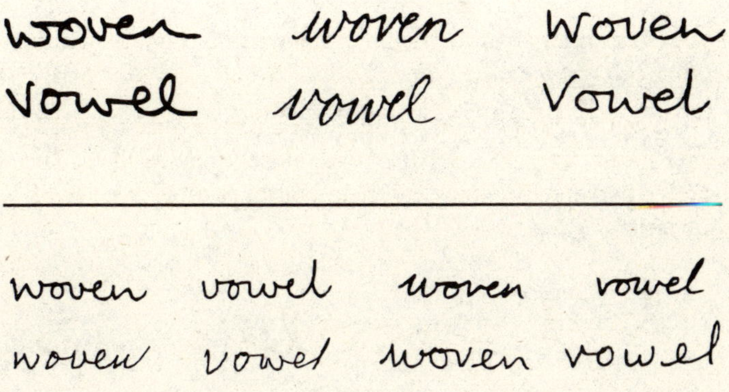

The more you look into other people's handwriting, the more interesting it becomes. See how these writers vary the letters **v** and **w** in the words 'vowel' and 'woven'. Sometimes they are round and sometimes spiky, both between and within the same word.

2

More about self-diagnosis

There are some problems that cannot be detected just by looking at a bit of writing. They leave no obvious trace. There are questions that you alone can answer. Ask yourself:

1 Is your writing good but not fast enough to do the job you want it to?

2 Could the way you hold your pen be affecting your writing?

3 Is it uncomfortable or even painful for you to write?

4 Does writing make you get a nasty lump on your middle finger?

5 Can you see what you are doing?

6 Are you relaxed when you are writing?

7 Are you left-handed?

8 Are you trying to write too fast?

9 Does your writing look different from one day to the next?

10 Do you really want quite a different style of handwriting?

Here is how to help yourself and where to find more information:

1 If your writing is good but not fast enough to do what you want it to, the answer is not so easy. Most people have two or three levels of writing. Keep your best writing for formal occasions.

Maybe you are such a neat and tidy person that you find it hard to write a faster, less exact hand. Writing is a means of communication. You must develop a more flexible attitude to it. Sometimes speed is more important than perfection.

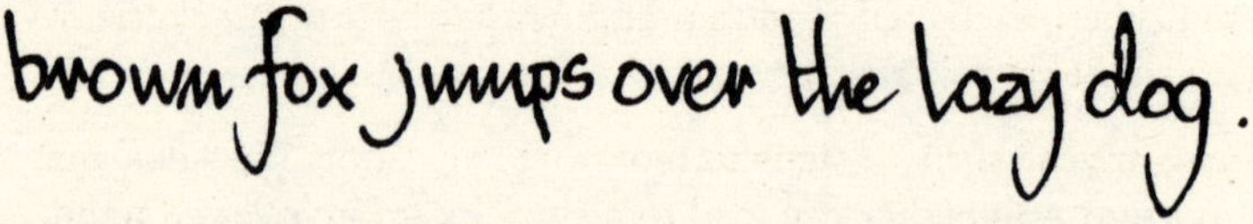

This teenager had been praised so much for his careful, attractive handwriting that he found it difficult to relax and develop a fast enough hand to pass examinations.

His writing hardly joins at all. He took five or six separate strokes to write the word 'little'. When he was shown a more flowing hand, it was difficult to persuade him that it was not 'untidy' but more mature.

What you write is probably more important than how it is written, though of course it must be legible. This certainly applies when writing essays for examinations. Quicker writing is obviously needed for taking notes too.

Remember, however, that you cannot write any faster than you can think. Some people are slow, deep thinkers, while others think faster than they can write.

So what can you do? First read through Chapter 3 about practical matters. Experiment with all kinds of pens. Many modern implements flow more freely than the traditional fountain pen. They help you to write faster. The result may be different but no less pleasing. A good letter is a good letter whether it is written with a ballpoint or a gold-tipped pen.

Next consider whether a slight tension of your hand is slowing you down. Try the relaxing exercises on page 28. Do a whole page of spirals until you are loosened up and feeling quite uninhibited, with your pen just skimming lightly over the paper. Then write a line as fast as you can – scribble it until it is barely legible.

Now compare it with your original perfect writing and try and analyse the differences. Maybe it slants forward more than before. This is not a bad thing. Slant is an indication of speed. You may have narrowed down a wide writing. On the other hand, you may have found that angular letters flow more freely with slightly rounded corners.

These are the sorts of signs to look for. They show the small but important points that can lead to a speedier, more relaxed hand.

In your case it will not necessarily help to retrain using our model (Chapter 8), but go on to consider whether your grip might be improved.

2 If you hold your pen awkwardly, it can stop your hand from moving and writing freely. You will have to judge for yourself whether it is worth the difficult task of retraining. The way you hold your pen might just be slowing you down. It can also make it difficult, if not impossible, for you to join your letters up at all. You can end up with a rather immature-looking writing.

Test to see whether your fingers can move freely when you hold your pen in your usual way. This is how you find out. Try the spiral exercises on page 28. You must be able to do them easily without moving your whole hand round and round. The way you place your fingers on the pen, or the way you twist your wrist, may be hindering you.

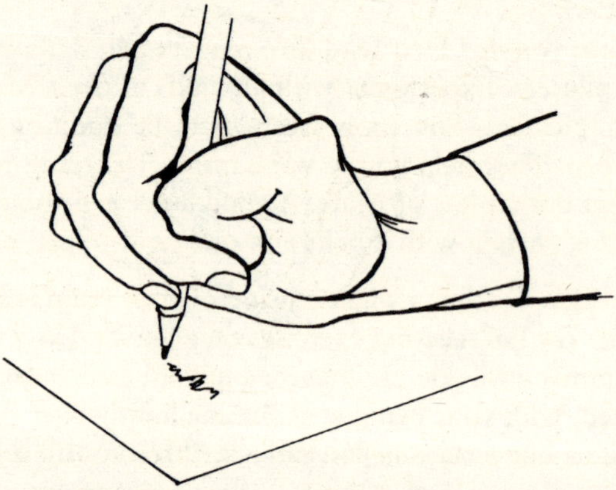

This kind of penhold makes it difficult to speed up your writing as you cannot move your fingers freely. It may also become painful after a while. This was drawn from an actual photograph.

Some adults have adapted to extraordinary ways of holding their pens. As long as it works for you, there is no need to change. But if you need help, read page 33.

3 If it is uncomfortable or even painful for you to write for any length of time, then you should consider altering the way you hold your pen. Even a slight twist of your wrist as you write can cause cramped muscles after a while. Then you end up with an aching arm or shoulder, which is a real problem for students at examination time. See pages 33–8 for instructions on retraining. You have the motivation. It is well worth trying.

4 If you have a nasty lump on your middle finger, this usually means that you been gripping your pen too hard. Quite likely you also press too hard when you write. Of course you must hold your pen firmly enough to control it. However, everything to do with writing must be flowing and relaxed. Read pages 27–8; try the relaxing exercises first. Make sure the pen handle is a comfortable shape and size for you. Then adjust the pressure of your fingers on the pen, and the pen on the paper, until everything moves smoothly.

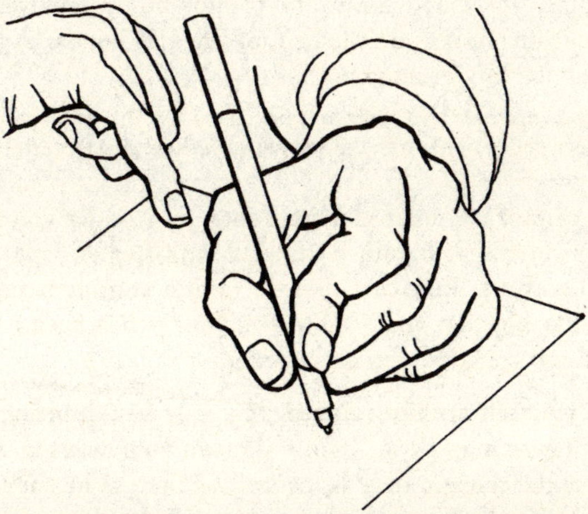

If your hand hurts when you write, first look at the way you hold your pen. Here the index finger is pressed hard on the pen. The writer needs to relax.

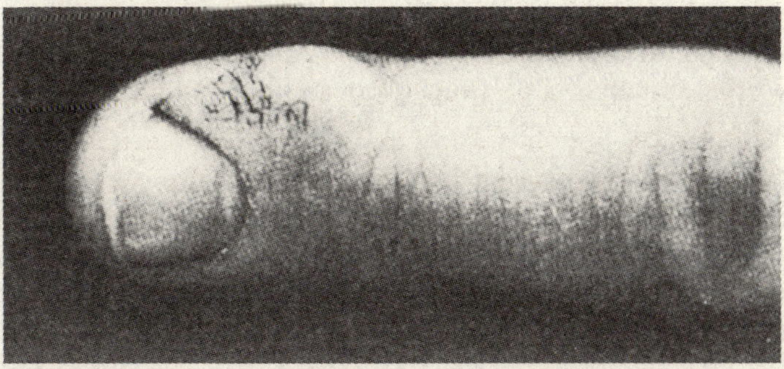

David's finger has grown a large callus because he holds his pen too tightly. These things can be avoided. Writing is not meant to be painful. As a calligrapher, however, he considers it a badge of honour!

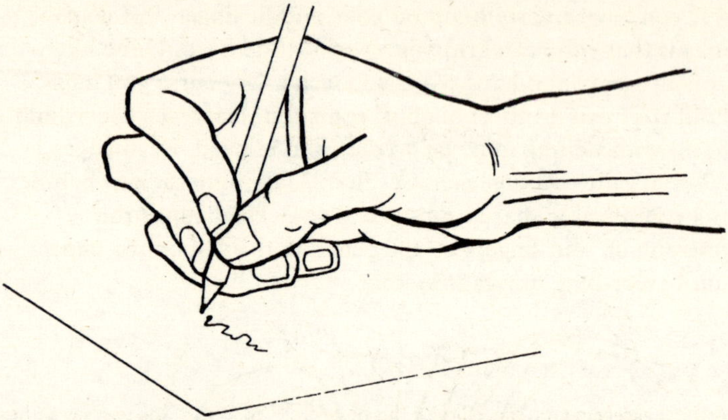

Here the two fingers are held stiffly together on the pen. This writer has quite long fingers. She might be better with the alternative penhold on pages 35 and 36.

5 If you cannot see what you are doing, no wonder you are having problems with your writing! Read Chapter 3 on practical matters. Take care that the light is coming from the correct side and that you are holding your pen in such a way that you *can* see what you are writing.

6 If you yourself are not relaxed, this may be inhibiting your writing. There may be no visible signs in your written work. Of course the tension may be caused by factors in your everyday life which are nothing to do with holding a pen. However, you can do something about the actual physical tension of writing. Page 27 tells you how to relax yourself. You may already know how to do this but never thought of applying the technique to the way you approach handwriting. Writing should be a pleasure; it can also be soothing and therapeutic.

7 If you are left-handed, Chapter 4 is especially for you. Check through all the general practical points too. There are some quite simple adjustments that you may never have thought about. They could help to solve problems that have troubled you for years.

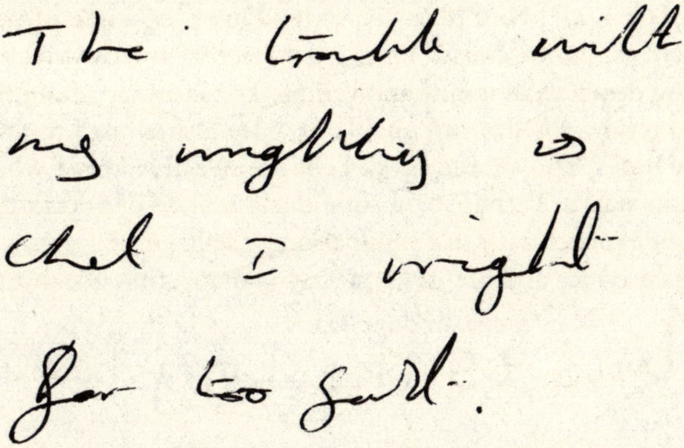

Are you exceeding the speed limit? This boy admits that he is. The text says: 'The trouble with my wrighting is that I wright far too fast.'

8 **If you are writing too fast** to be able to produce a legible hand, then you should read page 130 on the need for striking a balance between speed and legibility. You should also read Chapter 3 on practical matters. Experiment with pens and papers to find what suits you best. Perhaps you should try a broad-edge nib for a while to discipline your writing.

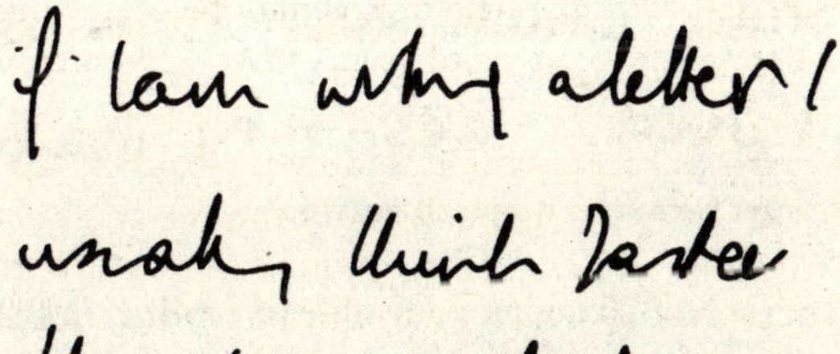

'If I am writing a letter I usually think faster than I can write [it] down' ... so do most of us, therefore we must strike a balance between speed and legibility.

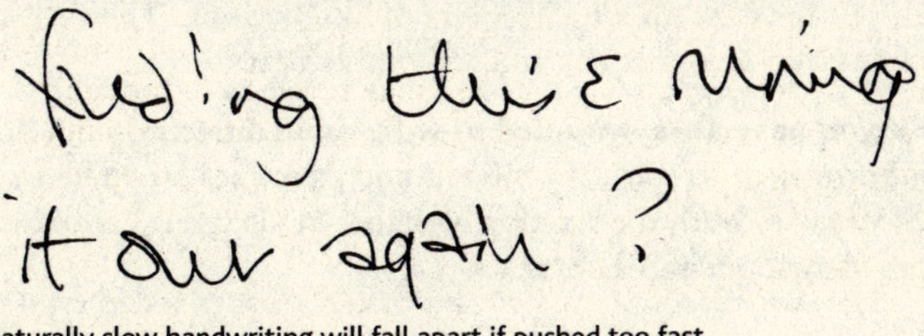

A naturally slow handwriting will fall apart if pushed too fast.

This book is all about how you write. However, some of your problems could be caused more by the actual words you choose to write down than your handwriting. For instance, if after all the exercises, you are still unable to write fast enough to take legible notes, you should try to be more selective about what you take down. Perhaps you should summarize in a form that you can expand later. In examinations it helps if you plan your essays carefully and are more precise in answering questions.

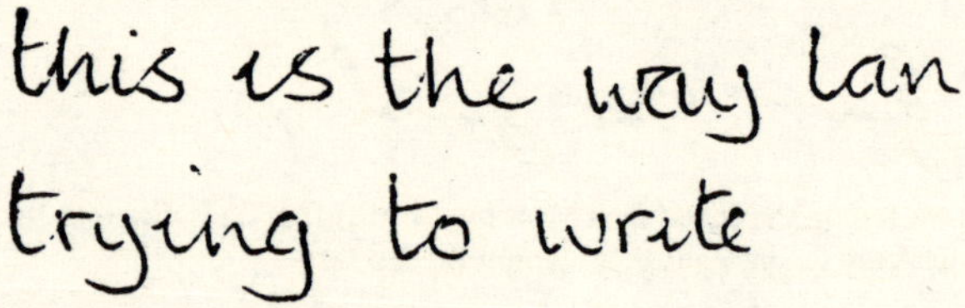

This girl's writing is at a changeable stage.

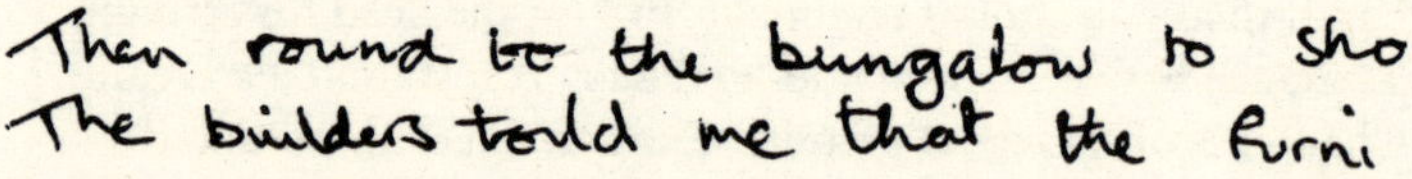

She writes one way one day and another the next.

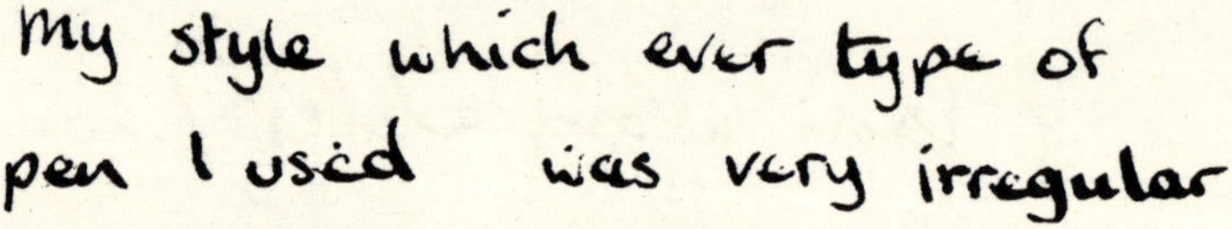

When she changes her pen her writing changes too.

9 If you are forever changing your style of writing, it may just mean that you are at a changeable stage yourself. If so, your writing will settle down when you do. What can you do? The rhythm and texture exercises in Chapter 7 can help you to establish your natural slant and letter shape. This book should help you to think about all aspects of handwriting. Then you can sort out what attracts you and works best for you.

10 If you have always wanted to write quite differently but do not know how to start, the models and examples are there to help you. Try both the training alphabet in Chapter 8 and the more formal one in Chapter 13.

If you have your own ideas about a new style and only need a method, then read page 77 on stroke-related sequences. It is easier to learn any alphabet, formal or informal, if you divide the letters into stroke-related groups. In some models the letters may be shaped differently so they may fit into other groupings. Working this out will help you with the alphabet you are choosing or changing to suit yourself.

3

Practical matters

A few practical points can make a lot of difference to the ease and quality of your handwriting. Most of them are common sense. However, it is amazing how often they are ignored, so use this chapter as a checklist before you start to work.

From time to time most of us scribble away curled up in an armchair or sitting in front of the fire. This is not good enough if you want to improve your writing.

1 You must have good light. Make sure that the shadow of your writing hand is not getting in the way. Try to sit so that the light is coming from your left if you are a right-hander. If you are a left-hander, of course, the light should come from your right.

2 You must be sitting comfortably, straight up and well balanced. Your chair should be the right height for your desk. You should be able to rest your arm comfortably on the writing surface. If the table is too high, then your shoulders are forced into an uncomfortable position. Be careful of chair arms that get in the way.

Some left-handers find it helpful to sit in a higher chair than a right-hander would choose.

3 The surface that you put your paper on is important too. You need to write on something resilient but smooth. The scratches and grain on an old wooden desk will come through the paper and disrupt your writing. A hard shiny table-top will make your pen skate over the surface of the paper and make your lines thin and scratchy too. A pad, or a few sheets of scrap paper underneath, will ensure that you have a sympathetic base to write on.

Have you tried writing on a sloping surface? It is very comfortable, and a great help if your hand is at all unsteady. The Victorians knew what they were doing – they used sloping writing desks. All you need is a board propped up on a couple of books.

4 Where should you place your paper? Your arm needs to be able to move freely if it is to work at its best. If you are right-handed, then your paper should be placed slightly to your right. If you are left-handed, it is even more important that your paper should be over to your left side.

One way of making a slanting writing surface is to use a loose-leaf book with the thin side nearer your body. This is useful in a college situation where most people have such books with them. This writer made a steeper slope using a second book. You will need to experiment to find the best angle for you to write at.

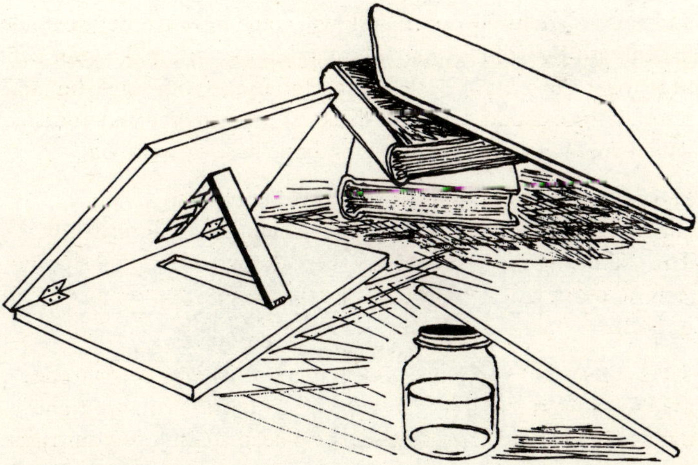

Three more ideas for making adjustable sloping surfaces for you to write on.

▶ It makes a lot of difference where you put your paper

With paper to the left, the arm awkwardly crosses the body. Writers cannot see what they have written.

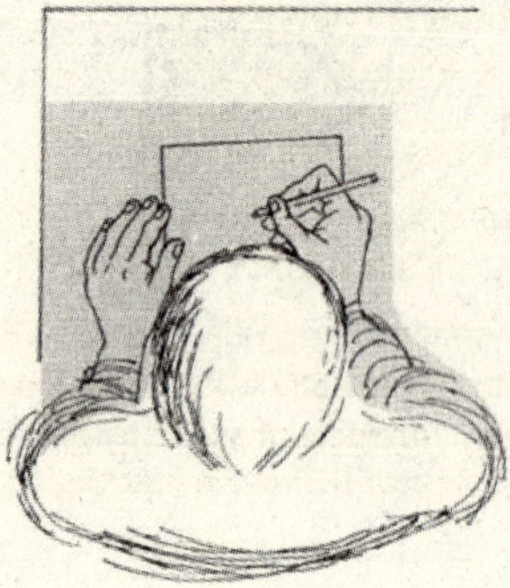

When the paper is placed centrally, the hand is tense and the elbow tucked in to the body.

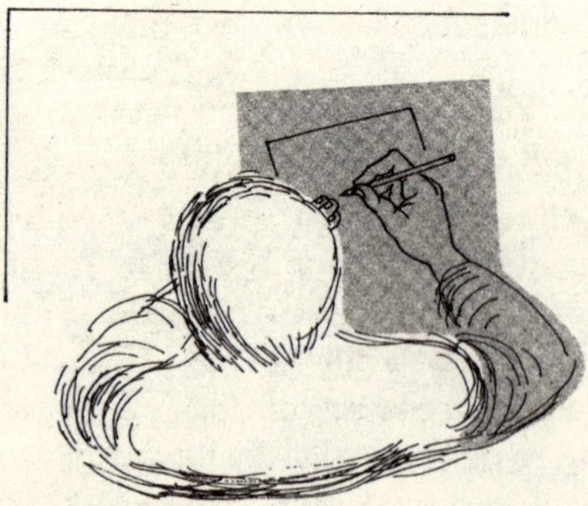

When the paper is placed to the writer's right side, the arm and hand can move freely.

Your arm has to stretch across your body if the paper is in the wrong position. You cannot see what you are doing for a start. Your movements are cramped and your writing will be cramped too. If you do not believe this, try putting your paper on the wrong side and see what happens. Far too many manuals say 'place the paper straight in front of you'. This may not be disastrous but it is not very helpful either.

You may like to work with your paper at a slant. You must experiment and see what is most comfortable for you. What works for one person is a positive hindrance to the next. If you are using a large sheet of paper, you may need to move it up as you progress. If the lines are long enough, it may be a help to move your paper from side to side: then you are ensuring that your arm is never over-stretched or cramped, and your writing benefits. These are all straightforward points, but the next one is not so easy.

5 You need to be relaxed. Tension causes jagged, uneven writing. You may leave out strokes or whole letters, and your writing can be pulled in all directions. If you get tense when trying to write carefully, it is not surprising. It may be that you are worried by the appearance of your handwriting, so trying hard to improve may make it even more impossible to relax. Whatever the cause – and there are plenty of reasons in all our lives – you must work consciously to relieve tension.

- Are your knees crossed? If so, uncross them.
- Are your shoulders hunched and tense? If so, relax them.
- Are you gripping your pen in a vice-like hold? Then ease up.

Take a couple of deep breaths and have a go at the scribble exercises (page 28) to loosen you up. They may look elementary but they are important: some pupils have found these relaxing exercises the most effective of the whole course and use them to loosen up before each writing session. You will find that you only need gentle pressure to let your pen glide over the paper. You may need to remind yourself to stop gripping so tightly. Check every few lines to make sure that you are not tightening up. If your fingers are gripping too hard, you can set up tensions that spread up your arm to your shoulder.

Writing should be a pleasure, not a strain.

6 What you write with and what you write on can make a whole lot of difference.

▶ Relaxing exercises

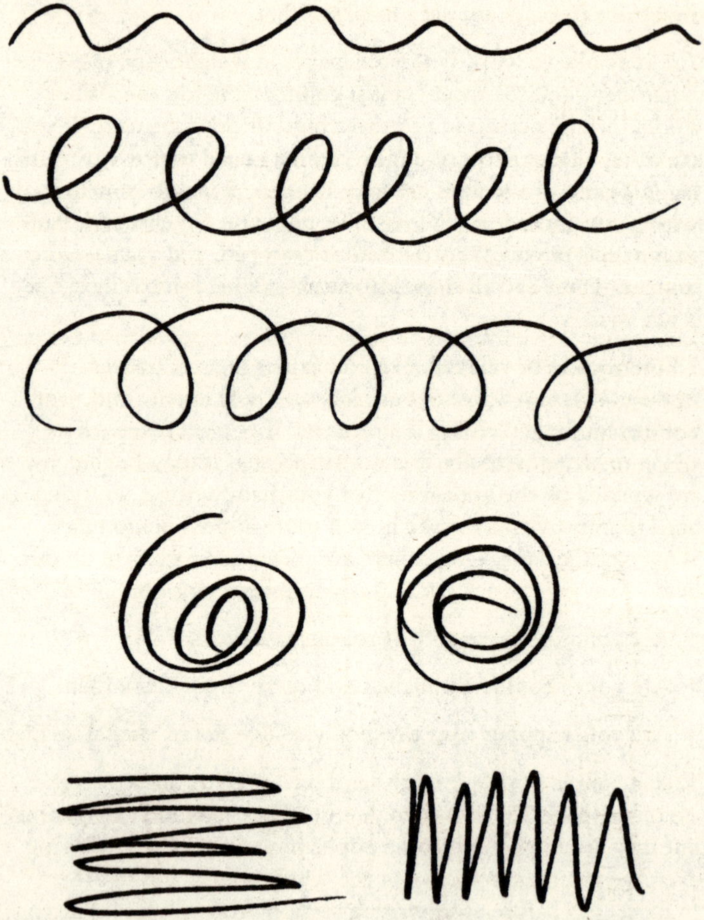

Free scribbles help you to loosen up. Do some and you will soon see how easily your pen should travel across the paper. Use them whenever you are tensed up, when retraining your grip, or when trying out a different pen.

Most of us at one time or another reach for the nearest ballpoint to make a quick note. You may cling to a favourite fountain pen that has great sentimental value. However, its nib or barrel may not have been chosen to suit you at all. You must experiment with all kinds of writing implements to see what suits you best. Try everything that you can lay your hands on, from an extravagant gold nib to the cheapest pen you can find. Walk into a good stationery shop and sample the wide variety of points and barrels that is available. The most expensive is not necessarily the best for you.

Next, try this experiment. Begin with a pencil with a very hard lead. Write out a simple sentence. Repeat the same sentence with a soft-leaded pencil and then with as many different pens as possible. You will notice how different they feel to write with, and you will see how your writing changes too.

Left-handers need as free-flowing a point as possible, so perhaps a fibre tip would suit them best. Other people say just the opposite: they find these pens run away with them. They lose control and their writing deteriorates, so they might prefer a traditional fountain pen or the discipline of a broad-edge nib.

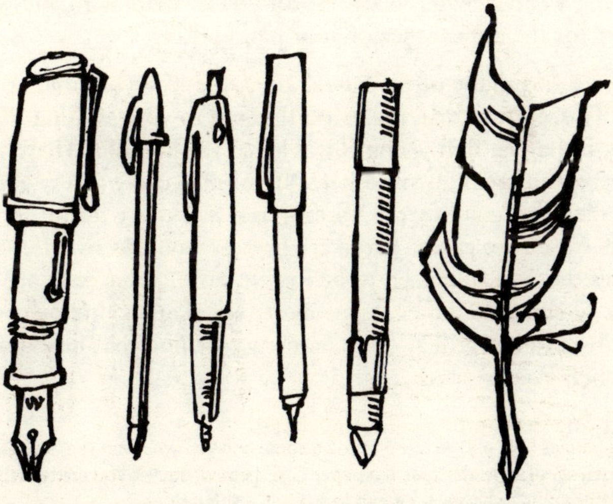

Try a variety of pens.

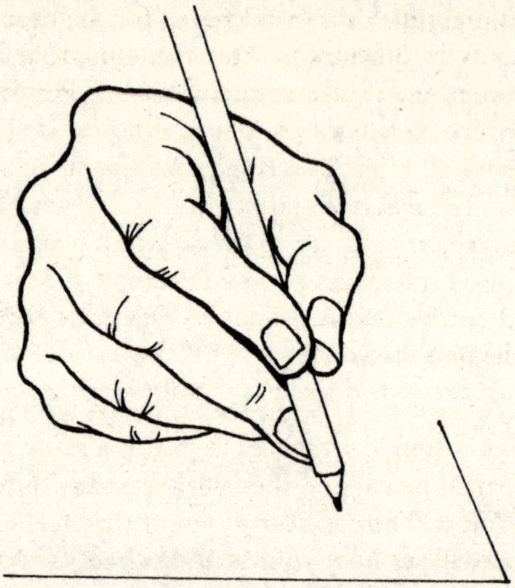

The traditional way of holding a pen is in a gentle pincer grip between your thumb and first finger, resting on the middle one. The angle of the pen to the paper will vary from person to person and from pen point to pen point. This penhold may not work as well with modern pens. See pages 35 and 36 for illustrations of an alternative penhold.

You must choose what is easiest for you to write with and what is best for the appearance of your handwriting.

The size and shape of the barrel affect the way you hold your pen. This, in turn, can make a difference to your writing. You must find a pen that is comfortable for you to hold. There are fat pens and medium-sized pens. If you like using a very slim pen, then you can buy the fibre-tip refills that are meant to fit inside expensive cases. There are barrels moulded to different shapes that are supposed to be easy to hold. Some pens are made of shiny materials, some matt. There are round pens and pencils, and hexagonal ones. Some people find that hexagonal ones help to correct their grip.

What one person likes, another hates.

Of course you need not keep to one pen only. Different tools suit different jobs: a ballpoint may be best for writing notes in an aircraft and a broad-edge nib best for a formal invitation.

The paper that you use also influences your writing. You write differently on a smooth surface than on a sheet with a slightly rough surface. Different pens behave differently, again depending on the quality of the paper.

That adds another permutation. When you have found a pen to suit your hand, find a paper to suit your pen. As always, you must choose for yourself: the most expensive paper need not be the best.

7 Lines. Well-spaced, even lines of writing create an immediate impression of clarity and legibility. Not everyone can achieve this. Their writing may sag in the middle of a line or droop at the end. It can go in a series of waves, perhaps colliding with the line above.

Few people are really happy writing important letters on lined paper.

If you have trouble keeping your writing in a straight line or level on the page, slip a sheet of ruled lines under your paper to guide you. It is quite easy to rule your own if the sheets that are usually supplied with writing pads are not spaced as you wish.

You do not want to get too dependent on guide lines. Use them only to train in good habits. It may not be your eye that is at fault. You may be writing in fits and starts along a page. You need to even out your pressure and intensity to maintain a good flow of writing. Then your lines will become more regular.

Some people may occasionally feel the need for four guide lines. If so, it is important that they use a size that is appropriate to their usual handwriting.

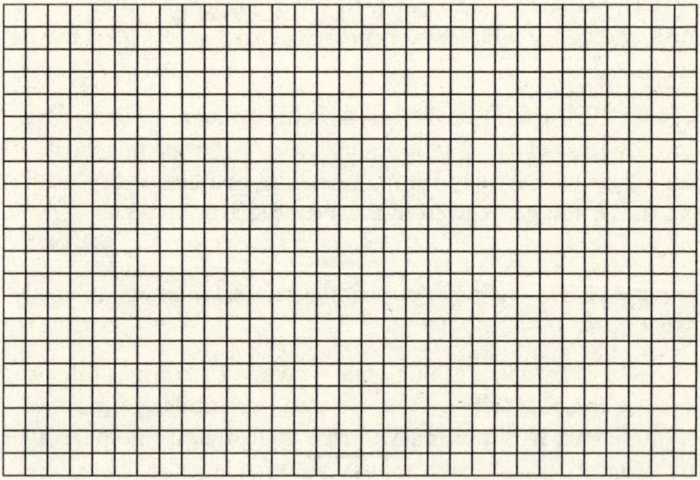

There is an alternative to ordinary lines – the faintly squared paper much used in continental Europe. This gives a certain amount of lateral support without imposing any particular size.

The relaxing exercises are meant to be free and uninhibited, so they are best done on unlined paper. For all the other exercises, however, use lined paper or, even better, squared paper. Initially you will need the assistance that lines give you, as they help train your hand and eye together to produce a disciplined hand. Then you should be able to do without them. Do not choose a pad with lines too close together, however.

Double lines ruled to fit your writing can be helpful in retraining really uncontrolled writing. More often they are used as a guide to enlarge a small writing or reduce a large one. Three or even four lines can help where there are problems with ascending or descending strokes. They will help to stretch or shrink your writing as required, depending on how they are spaced.

Carefully measured lines are a help. Badly ruled ones are a hindrance, as your eye automatically obeys them.

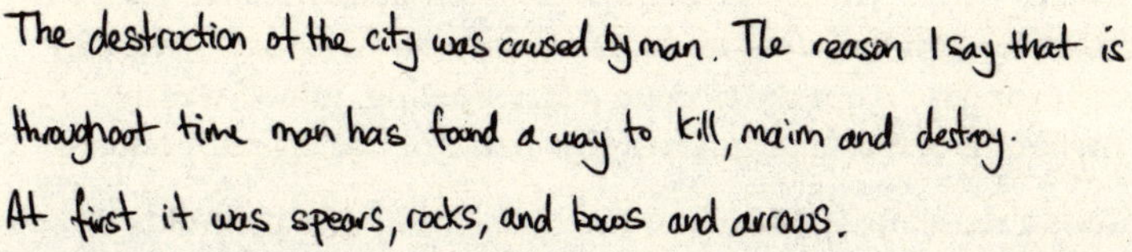

Would some widely spaced double lines help this person with very small writing to write larger? Very unlikely. Relaxing exercises would be of more help.

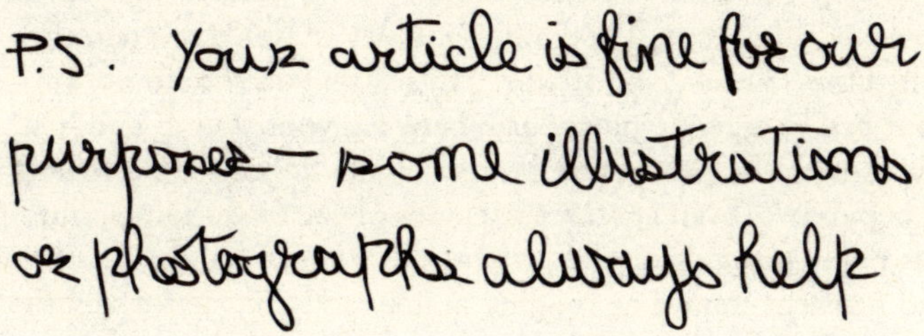

Would double lines spaced closely together help this writer to write smaller? Not at all. He has slight co-ordination problems and finds it difficult to do the intricate movement that would enable him to reduce the size of his writing.

8 The way you hold your pen will affect the letters that you write. This is the most complicated issue that we have to deal with in this part of the book, because so many factors are involved. It is your hand that writes. Letters are the visible trace of a hand movement when that hand holds a pen and the pen is in contact with the paper. It is not only the fingers that need to be considered, but the rotation of the wrist. This determines whether you write with your hand on edge or slightly flattened. The rotation often controls the slant of your writing, whereas the position of the fingers on the pen, in particular which digit is nearest to the pen point, is more likely to affect the proportions of your letters. Experiment yourself, then you will feel and see what it is all about.

How you position your arm, and therefore your hand, is dependent on where you have got used to placing your paper. Where you place your paper is dependent on whether you were helped to work out the best position for yourself, and had plenty of space on the desk earlier on, when you were learning to write. You may have become accustomed to writing with an unconventional penhold. If it works for you, then it does not matter what it looks like to anyone else. Some awkward penholds, however, can make it painful for you to write. More often they can stop you from developing a free-flowing, joined writing. Awkward penholds can slow you down or distort your letters.

Today there are more and more unconventional penholds to be observed in schools, shops, offices or wherever people can be seen at work with pen and paper. There is a logical explanation as to why this should be happening, but no golden rules about how to deal with it. The traditional way of holding a pen is called the 'tripod grip'. It works this way: you should hold your pen in a gentle pincer grip between your thumb and first finger, with the pen resting on the middle finger. (Some writers of copybooks even specify the angles of the finger joints, but this really depends on the proportions of your hand.) Your hand and forearm should be roughly in line, and your hand slightly flattened. These instructions work well for traditional pens or pencils, but not so well for modern pens. Ballpoints, rollerballs, fibre- or felt-tipped pens only work when they are held in a much more upright position. Trouble can start when you try to adapt a conventional penhold to deal with a modern pen.

There are roughly three different ways that people go about trying to get their pen upright:

1 You can squeeze your pincer grip very tightly. This should alter the elevation of the pen but can be very painful – even more so when you have to work at speed.

2 You can stop the thumb from pressing so much and allow the index finger to push the pen upright. In moderation this works well, as the thumb slides on to the top of the pen. If the thumb goes too far over, an inefficient wrapped-round kind of penhold develops. This limits some of the movements and therefore some of the strokes that are needed to make up our letters.

3 You can push more with the thumb, but this is not a good idea as the thumb begins to bend backwards. It usually results in using at least two fingers coming in to action

against it. The pen comes upright but you end up with a very stiff, inefficient, limiting and eventually painful solution.

Try all these methods out for yourself. This is the best way to understand the dilemma we find ourselves in today.

There is another way out of this muddle. Maybe we should set about finding a penhold more suited to modern pens. They are here to stay so we cannot ignore the situation. Throughout the history of writing whenever the writing implement altered so did the prescription of how to hold it. At the same time, those involved understood that inevitably the letterforms would also alter. Sometimes the letters altered first and the pens and penholds followed, but that makes no difference to the argument. Today our priorities are clear. We need to write fast as well as legibly. We must find ways of holding modern pens that will enable us to write without pain. Our hands were not designed to hold a small stick and make very accurate marks at speed and under stress. We also need to encourage efficient letters suited to modern pens. Unless we begin to do something sensible about both letters and penholds, we will contribute more to the demise of handwriting than the coming of the computer has done.

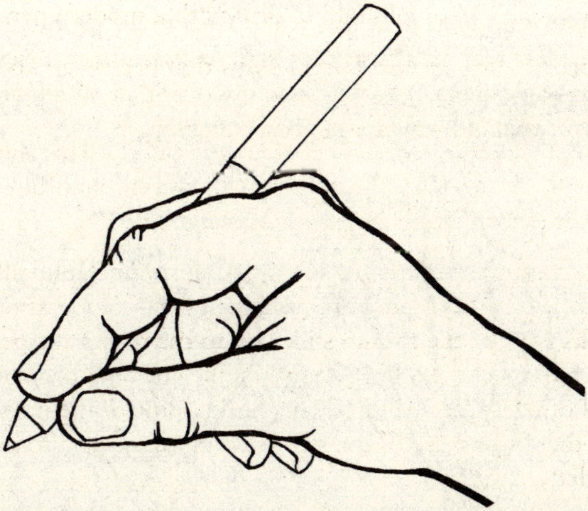

This is an alternative way of holding a pen. It works well with modern pens that need to be more upright in order to work properly. You place the pen between the web of your index and middle fingers, and then arrange your fingers comfortably on the barrel of the pen.

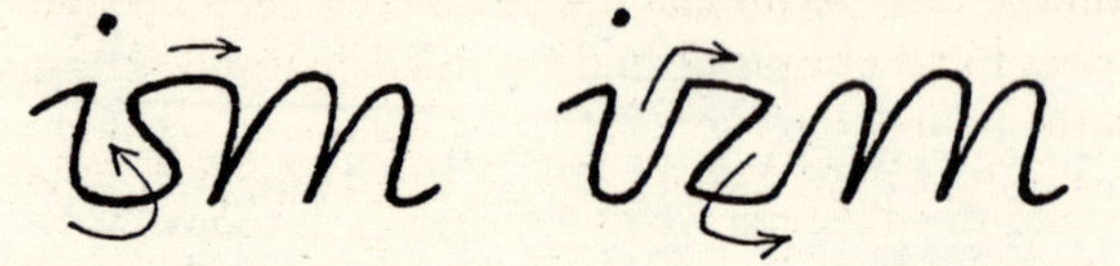

The ballpoint has caused a great change in writing. The pen will move with the same ease in any direction. It is as simple to write an ***s*** upwards as down, and probably quicker. But would it be recognizable?

The alternative penhold illustrated here sorts out several problems at once. The way of holding the pen between the web of the index and middle finger allows any type of pen to be held at any angle. It is restful for the fingers – they are no longer in opposition to each other so the muscles are able to work in unison. Much of the tension that resulted from the tripod grip (in other than very relaxed circumstances) now disappears. This alternative penhold suits left-handers as well as those who write with their right hands (see pages 45–7). It was researched by a Belgian neurologist called Callewaert and his findings were reassuring; however, he by no means invented it. Egyptian scribes have been depicted as using a similar hold, and it is likely that Roman scribes also employed it to write a particular form of letters called rustics. Many adults worldwide hold their pens this way. Observe the penholds of world leaders and royalty as they sign treaties under the eye of the television camera. You will soon discover that, as a user of the alternative penhold, you are in good company.

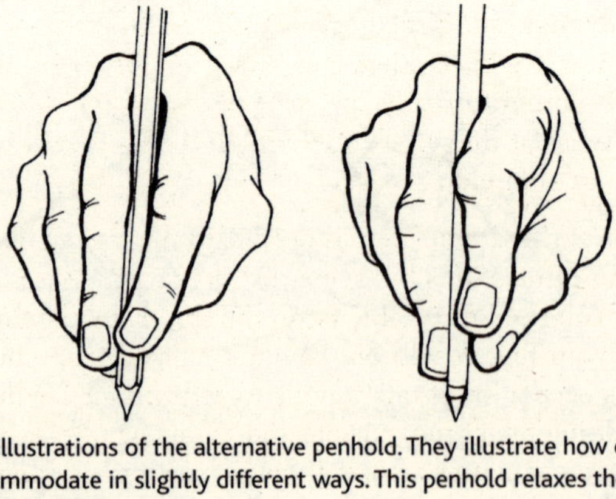

Two more illustrations of the alternative penhold. They illustrate how different hands accommodate in slightly different ways. This penhold relaxes the hand and is good for relieving cramp.

It is still too early to proclaim that this alternative penhold is an answer to all our problems, but it is safe to say that it has solved the pain and tensions of many a student at examination time, as well as those suffering from more serious conditions.

Now that you understand more about the hand, the matter of the rotation of the wrist needs explaining. Whether you write with your hand on edge or slightly flattened is up to you. It does not matter a bit unless it is causing you trouble. Many artistic people have a wonderfully relaxed control of the pen with their hand on edge. It is the very factor that enables them to have efficient and often enviably beautiful handwriting. However, if you are tense, this same 'on edgeness' may cause trouble. If the hand is on edge, then the fingers are further from the point of the pencil as it touches the paper. One solution that many people take is to place two fingers on the pen to steady it. This may work well or, on the other hand, it may not. Two other problems can arise when writers who have their hands on edge come under pressure. Sometimes they press down on their hand so hard that it cannot move along the line. This is most frustrating. The other problem is just as bad. The writer may tip the hand forward in order to be nearer the paper. That causes the wrist to twist so that the hand comes above the line of writing. You are then pushing downward (towards yourself) with a jerky movement of the wrist to write a stroke, instead of gently guiding the pen with your fingers. This may make your writing slope backwards. It certainly makes it difficult to join up. See the examples on pages 143–4. Right-handers end up with another trouble that many left-handers already suffer from: writing with even the slightest twist of the wrist can be painful or set up cramp in your arm or shoulder.

It is important that you should be able to move your fingers freely. You can test this by trying the relaxing exercises on page 28. You need to be able to do the spirals by moving your pen with your fingers without having to move your whole hand. There has been a lot of talk among experts about the difference between using finger movements and whole hand movements. Basically, it is a matter of size. If you have small writing, you need to move your hand less. Copperplate and some of the cursives derived from it do use more of a hand movement. The models coming into general use now need more agile fingers. This brings us to the next consideration: speed.

These triangular plastic grips fit over pens and pencils. They are comfortable to write with and keep your fingers in the correct position.

The points of modern writing implements work differently from the traditional fountain pen nib. They can move in any direction equally easily, making it easier to write fast. You do not want to be held back by a grip that stops your hand from moving freely enough to take advantage of this because, as for most people, speed is a top priority today.

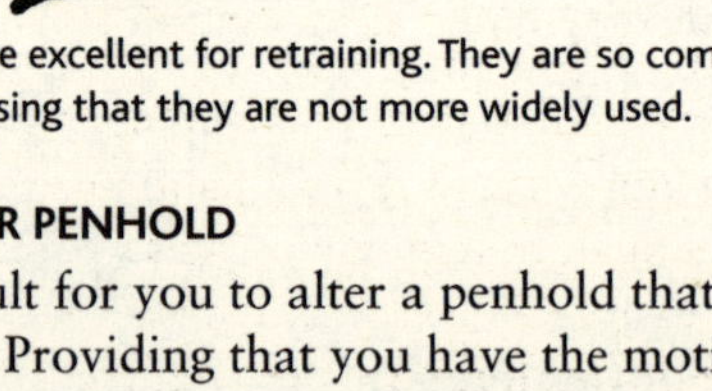

Triangular pencils are excellent for retraining. They are so comfortable to write with that it is surprising that they are not more widely used.

CHANGING YOUR PENHOLD

It may be difficult for you to alter a penhold that you have used for a long time. Providing that you have the motivation, you *can* do it. First you need to analyse what you are doing wrong. Then you need to realize that, in order to alter your penhold and the position of your hand, you may need to reconsider where you place your paper. These two issues – paper position and penhold – are so interrelated that, except for the most minor alterations, you almost always have to work on both matters together. As you experiment, not only will you probably solve your own problems but you will also wonder why it had all blown up into such a big issue. That can be explained relatively simply. Everything about handwriting soon becomes automated. It has to so that, once learned, you can forget about the act of writing and concentrate on what you want to say. If you develop and automate any particular writing posture, then all the muscles in your hand, arm and even down your back become used to working together in a particular pattern. It is all so automatic that, even when the pain caused by an awkward posture becomes intense, the writer does not realize that in fact that pain is self-inflicted. 'Writing posture' is a good term to introduce here.

It combines the way you sit in relation to your chair, the relation of your chair to the table and the position of your paper on the table. These factors influence how freely your arm is able to function which, in turn, can influence how your penhold is able to develop. When you need to alter any part of your writing posture, then a whole set of muscles has to be retrained. This is not easy to do unless there is real motivation. The important thing for you to assess is how important the alteration is for you. It is only you who must be considered, not any advisor, or teacher or friend. If it is necessary to alter some aspect of your posture, then you must have convinced yourself. Somehow you will find the necessary motivation to change.

Sometimes the alteration is minimal. Those who would like to keep to a traditional penhold might find relief from minor strain, or lumps on the middle finger, by using a triangular plastic grip. These are readily available from educational suppliers. If you are right-handed and want to relax a hand position that is on edge, it may be enough to remind yourself to flatten your hand so you can see a couple of knuckles as you write. Your hand will then be in line with your forearm and your pen below the line of writing. This will not be enough to help left-handers. Their solutions are discussed in detail in the next chapter. It will not be enough for right-handers either if the twisted, over-the-top hand position is complicated by having the paper in the wrong place. They will need to start by moving their paper over to their right side. Some writers will find relief from a sloped board to write on. Others will find a change to the alternative penhold is often a solution, particularly at times of stress.

Any alteration in writing posture may feel strange at first, so do not expect to write long passages straight away. Start with some relaxing exercises, then some repetitive stroke and letter sequences before launching into full-scale sentences. Do not be surprised if you tend to slip back into your old ways. You need to remind yourself from time to time to keep to the new posture. Gradually it will come to feel natural and you will realize how much more freely you are writing.

4

Help for left-handers

We should not assume that handwriting is always a problem for left-handers. Many of the best architects, artists and sculptors are left-handed. They, and many others, had no problems with handwriting. However, a proportion of left-handers do have difficulties, and it is to those that this section is addressed.

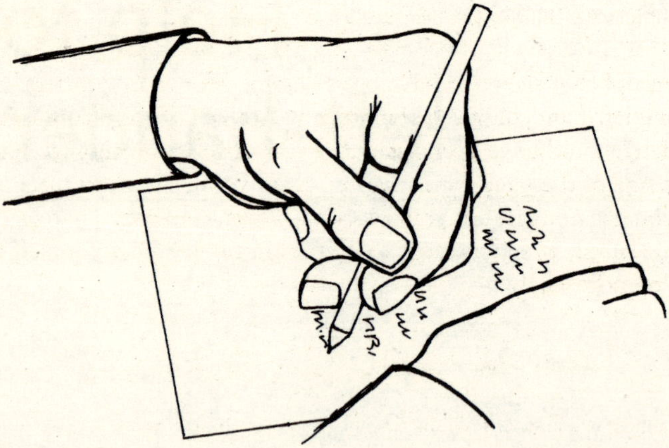

Many left-handers adopt an over-the-top (inverted) hand position. This often happens because they were not shown how to place the paper over to their left side when they learned to write. It is not easy to alter your writing posture. The first step is to move the paper and then experiment with it at different angles.

A set of practical suggestions is provided here that should help you. If you had been helped in this way when you started to write at school, it is probable that you would have had fewer difficulties today. There are, however, more serious problems for some left-handers and it is only fair that these should also be given prominence. A sad consequence of ignoring left-handers' needs (dare we say rights) means that they may have underachieved in much of their academic work. This can come about because of continuous uninformed criticism about the slant, quality, non-adherence to the school model or even smudging that sometimes appears in a left-hander's writing. When you are criticized for everything that you write, is it surprising that you produce less and less written work?

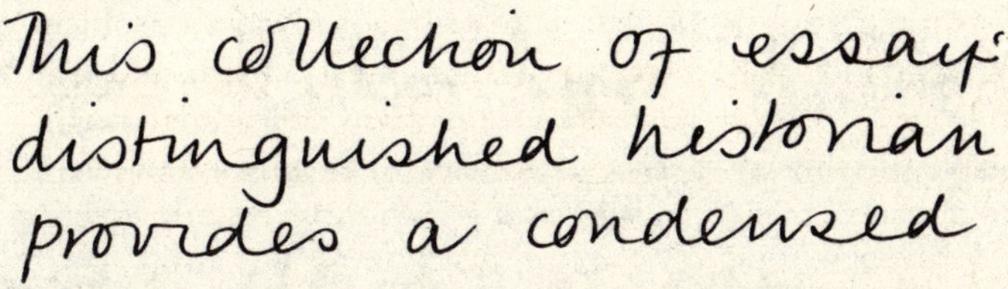

Left-handers do not necessarily have problems with handwriting. This is a beautifully free-flowing left-handed cursive.

Our alphabet seems to have been designed for right-handers – being left-handed, maybe Hebrew or Arabic (written from right to left) would have been easier for you. As it is, starting from the left side of the page, you cover up what you have just written. If you are not careful, your work also gets smudged. There are quite simple practical steps that you can take to help yourself to write more easily.

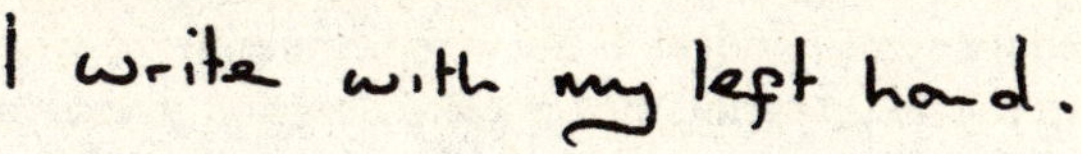

An almost unjoined writing. The writer has an over-the-top grip.

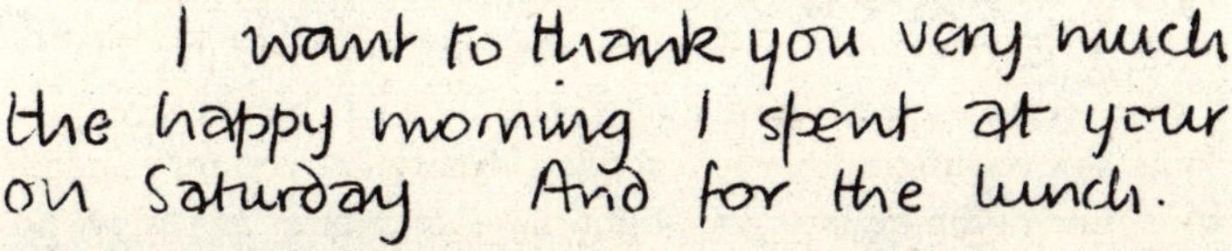

A pleasant, fluent left-handed script.

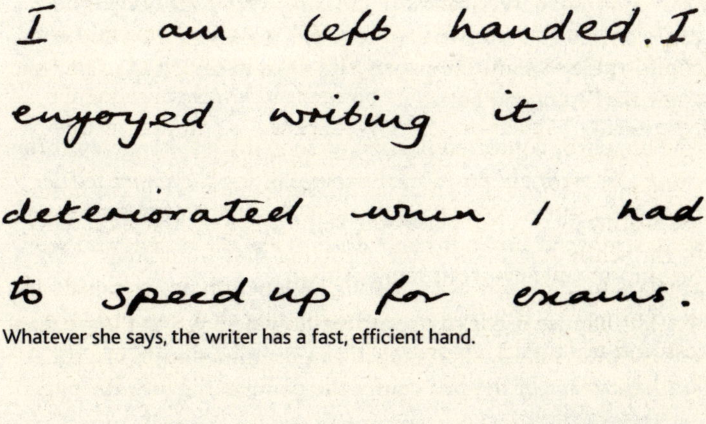

Whatever she says, the writer has a fast, efficient hand.

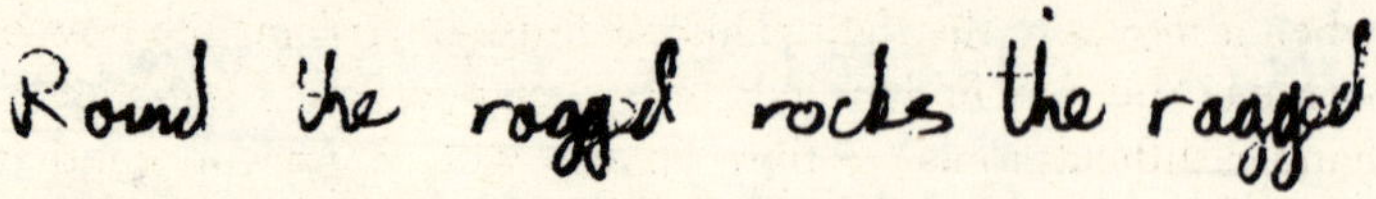

Rather a cramped hand. The writer sat awkwardly and could not move his arm freely.

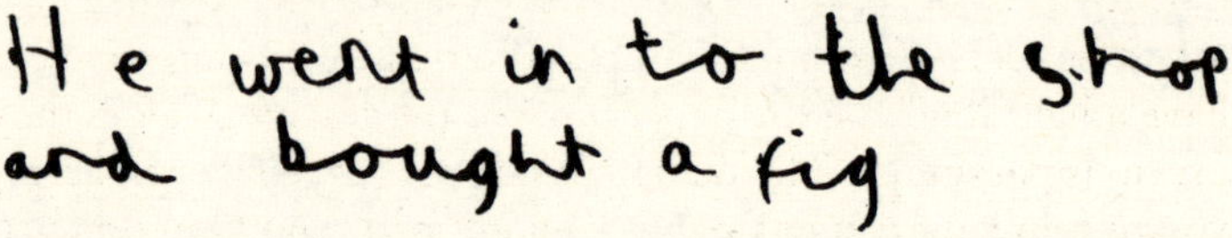

This left-hander's awkward grip distorts his letters. Strokes are pushed from the top. It slows him down, too.

Steps to writing more clearly

1 Try to sit so that the light comes over your right shoulder. This way you will not get the shadow of your writing hand on your work. Unfortunately, far too many classrooms and offices are organized for right-handers. If the worst comes to the worst, you may have to end up facing the opposite direction to everyone else.

2 You need to sit towards the right side of your desk or table, leaving plenty of room for your left hand and arm to move freely. Keep that side of your desk clear of books and papers. If two people have to share a desk, choose a left-hand place or try to share with another left-hander. Otherwise, you may spend your time bumping into your right-hand neighbour as you work.

3 Place the paper to your left side on the table. This lets your arm move freely without crossing over your body. You can see what you are writing, too, this way. You may find it comfortable to slant the paper. You must experiment to find the angle that suits you best.

The hunched, contorted posture of so many left-handers is often caused by wrongly positioned paper. Putting the paper in the right position lets you sit up straight. A change of posture may seem strange at first but you will soon feel the benefit and see the improvement in your handwriting.

4 A left-hander needs to **use as free-flowing a writing implement as possible.** A hard, sharp pencil can be quite disastrous: the left-hand slant of the pen causes the point to dig into the paper

when it moves to the right. This obviously interrupts the flow of writing. You may find an italic nib, even one slanted for a left-hander, difficult to use. A fibre tip may work better for you than a conventional pen. It is all a matter of trying out the different points and seeing what suits you.

5 Left-handers often hold their pen too tightly. It is important to have a light touch on the paper too, for the reason given in the previous paragraph. The relaxing exercises (page 28) will help you to **grip your pen less tightly and not press too hard on the paper as you write.**

6 You may need to **hold your pen a little higher up the barrel** than a right-hander in order to see what you are doing. If you have trouble remembering this, a strategically placed rubber band will help to remind you until it feels more natural. Try a higher chair. You may find it easier to see over the top of your hand as you write.

7 A left-hander may have even more trouble than a right-hander **finding a comfortable, efficient penhold.** Read first the section on the way to hold your pen on page 33. Some of the general matters there might also affect you. For a start, the alternative penhold works well for left-handers too. If you have a penhold that works for you, stick to it even if other people make rude remarks about it. If you are quite comfortable with an over-the-top hand position, if it does not slow you down or distort your letters, then there is no reason for you to change. If you are not happy with your penhold, then start experimenting right now.

The traditional way for a left-hander to hold a pen is in a gentle pincer grip between the thumb and index finger, resting it on the middle finger. This does not always work well with modern pens so feel free to experiment if you are having trouble.

Remember all the time that penhold, paper position and letters are all inextricably involved. Alter one and the others will also need to alter. If you want to alter an inverted hand position, you must first move your paper over to your left side. To our way of thinking a wrong paper position is the main cause of this penhold. With paper straight in front of them, young writers cannot see what they are writing about without twisting the wrist or their whole body (or both). When you have altered the paper position, then try playing about with different slants, to find one that is comfortable for you. Together the new position and slant will help to bring your hand round to below the line of writing, or at least in from the side rather than as it was – on top of the line of writing.

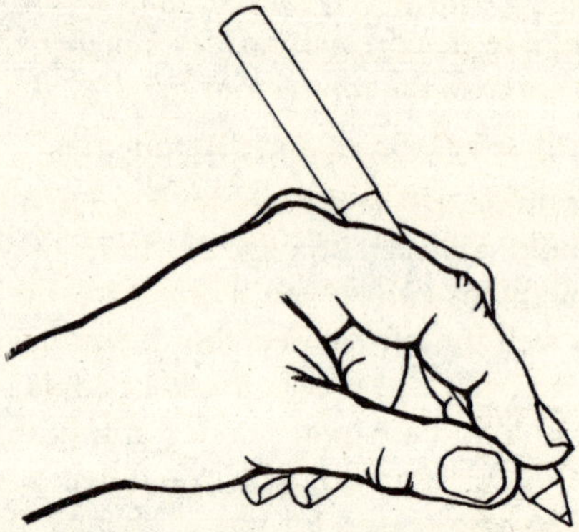

The alternative penhold works well for left-handers. Try it. Place the pen between the index and middle fingers and then arrange your fingers comfortably on the barrel of the pen.

Then it is time to find out the best way to place your fingers on the pen. You can try the traditional way – more or less a reversal of the traditional right-handed penhold. Hold the pen in a gentle pincer grip between the thumb and index finger, resting it on the middle finger. But this is not the only way – there is no guarantee that this will suit you. There is the influence of modern pens to contend with for you as well as for right-handers. Try the alternative penhold or any variation that works well for you and allows you to write freely, without discomfort. Any alteration will feel odd at first. A free penhold will alter your handwriting too. It should look much more relaxed. Do not mistake this new freer writing for untidiness. Do a few of the relaxing exercises first, then some letter sequences, and be patient. These things take time to settle down.

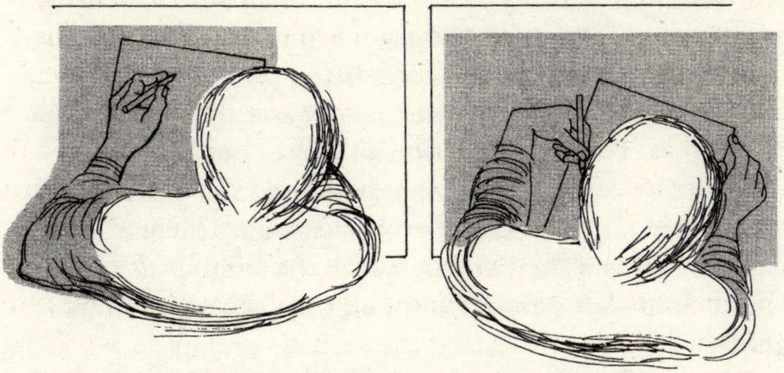

Left-handers need to place the paper to their left side so that they can see what they are doing without having to twist the wrist.

These are all fairly simple points but they can make a left-hander's life much easier. They can also be extremely useful for right-handed people who have lost the use of their natural writing hand through illness or accident and have to learn to use their left hand.

Plastic pen grips help to keep your fingers in place. They should be placed a little higher up the pen for a left-hander than for a right-hander.

Some other issues are not so easy to explain, but the next few paragraphs may help some of you to understand, if not cure, your personal difficulties. When tested, left-handers usually show that they find it easiest to draw a line, or to write, from right to left. It is usually easier for them to draw a circle in a clockwise direction. While most right-handers cross their letter **t** from left to right, most left-handers do it the other way round – from right to left. Just try it. This simple experiment illustrates one problem that shows up at different levels. At the simplest level it occurs when joining from letters with a crossbar – **f** and **t**. A right-hander can go straight across the crossbar and on to the next letter. The left-hander whose crossbar prefers to go in the opposite direction, has ended up at the wrong place and needs to pull the pen back to restart the next letter. This takes longer. Then there is another issue that usually, but not always, gets better with age. Young left-handers often want to start to write at the 'wrong' side of the paper. Then their writing all comes out reversed. The same can also happen in a separate word. Some left-handers start to write at the end and go backwards. Teachers may not even notice this if they do not watch the child in the act of writing. Some left-handers form all their separate letters from right to left. This means that they always end up in a position that makes joined letters impossible. Again, this can only be spotted by watching the writer in action.

All this could be explained when children start school, and special attention paid to left-handers' directionality. Great care should be taken to help young left-handers deal with the movement of the strokes that make up our letters. Once any movement becomes automated, it is increasingly hard to alter. What about you as an adult? Those people who have extreme difficulty with the direction of writing may have great difficulty travelling from left to right along the page in every way – in scanning to read, in separate letters, or in whole words. They often go in the wrong direction when copying from the blackboard, or in other situations where they have to keep looking up from their work, frequently stopping and starting to write. People who have this problem can explain how it feels. When they write slowly and neatly, this urge to go right round a letter and backwards along the line is almost uncontrollable. Sometimes the momentum gathered when they write fast helps to overcome this problem – but, if they write fast, they may be criticized for being untidy or illegible.

Some letters are even more difficult than others for you to write. When adult left-handers find it impossible to alter the way they go round an **o**, then the solution may be just never to join it up. It is the joining that distorts letters that move other than the traditional way. Top joins – those that slide so easily across a line of joined **o**'s or **w**'s for a right-hander – are likely to be the hardest for you. Then leave them out as well as those that go over the top and back when they join to round letters. Concentrate on those that work well for you – probably those that join on the baseline. Too many joins are a strain in anyone's hand, so the continuously joined cursives, still taught in some countries, are particularly difficult for left-handers. Do not be bullied at any age about the slant of your writing. It is easier for some left-handers to write at a slight backward slant. You can adjust this to a certain extent by slanting the paper, but does it really matter so much? In countries that insist that every child slopes his or her handwriting forward, all that happens is that many of them have to adopt an over-the-top hand position in order to do so. What is worse, an uncomfortable writing posture for life or a consistent personal handwriting with a slight backward slant? Some of us feel so strongly about this that we suggest that young left-handers should have a slightly different model to copy. Why should they always have to adhere to a slant and perhaps a model that is specially difficult for them? It is little wonder that some young left-handers become rebellious while others become depressed by the constant ignoring of their needs.

Research into left-handers' hand positions

Most people think that it is impossible to alter the over-the-top hand position that is adopted by some left-handers. A survey with 100 secondary school children proved otherwise. Of the ten left-handers in the sample, three of them had managed to change when it became painful and slowed them down at an age when they needed to write faster. They demonstrated how they had to alter their paper position. Their script improved too, and was much more relaxed and flowing.

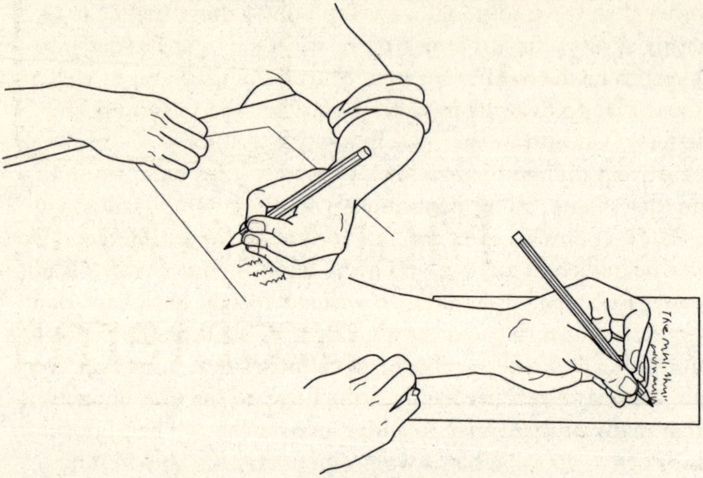

This student changed spontaneously from an over-the-top (inverted) hand position to a conventional one when she found that the twisted position of her wrist became painful and stopped her from writing fast enough.

5

More serious problems

Anyone at any time can have an accident that temporarily or permanently damages the writing hand. There are a few simple rules that make all the difference in those circumstances. When you need to learn to write with your other hand, remember:

1 Change the paper over to the side of the altered writing hand, and experiment to find the best position and angle for you.

2 Get a new pen, preferably something like a fibre tip, that will glide easily over the paper and will not smudge. Your old and treasured fountain pen will have been worn down to suit the other hand.

3 Some letterforms may need to be simplified. When changing to the left hand, the letters **s** and **f** are usually the ones that need this most.

When you have to change from one hand to the other, then the angle and perhaps the whole flavour of your writing may alter too. Try not to let this worry you. If it is necessary, then you will get used to it. You will also have the motivation to practise, so gradually you will become consistent and confident in your new handwriting. There are many other conditions that affect handwriting – strokes, many different neurological problems, as well as that little-understood condition, writer's cramp. All too often the therapists ignore writing when they retrain what are called 'daily living skills'. If you cannot sign your name or fill in a form, then you are dependent on someone else to conduct all your business for you. There is more to it than that. Your writing is the way you present yourself to the world, and your signature is especially important. Computers are here to help us, but they do not do the same thing for the patient. There is another advantage to this argument. If you can persuade a stroke patient, for instance, that the damaged hand is retrainable and quite capable of making a mark with a bit of help, then the motivation to improve can be dramatic. Patients will practise their name over and over again, with the reassuring visible feedback of the trace in front of them. In this way they are improving their hand function for other actions such as eating. Signature writing is much more stimulating and positive than picking up buttons and replacing them in a box, which is the usual exercise for damaged hands.

A tremor needs special help. To start with, a sloping surface to write on is a great help. Anything will do – in bed, a cushion at an angle under a writing pad; in the wheelchair, a piece of hardboard or even firm polystyrene balanced against a table. On a desk or table all you need is a large atlas or piece of hardboard propped up on a couple of books. When you find out how much this helps, you can consider something more permanent. It is quite simple to have a slanting board made, with some non-slip material underneath to make it steadier. Make use of both of your hands. The undamaged one can support and guide the damaged one until the magic moment when it can work alone.

For those who may be guiding patients, remember that the style of writing is irrelevant. Do not use children's copybooks. Help your patients to make whatever slant, size or shape of mark or stroke that comes most easily to them. Then work the 'mark' or stroke gradually into whatever letter that particular patient can manage at that moment. Administer large doses of praise! Do not stick to capital letters as some people do, thinking that they are easier. If the writer used to join some letters, then encourage him or her to do so again. Separate letters need a lot of repositioning which is difficult with a tremor. Joins give the hand and the writing stability – although the result may look shaky at first.

Those with degenerative conditions can be helped to prolong their ability to write with quite simple techniques. Modern pens that glide across the paper maximize any movement in the hand and arm. Smooth paper helps too. A change of technique using different muscles can also succeed, as it did in the case of a patient with multiple sclerosis. She had lost the strength in her fingers and wrist, but she retrained in a whole-arm movement that uses more of the shoulder muscles. She returned to the copperplate writing of her school days, and ten years after is still writing happily.

Finally, we need to look at that complex condition known as writer's cramp. This occurs when writers find that their body refuses to work for them in that one action alone. It has long baffled neurologists, the specialists who are most frequently consulted. However, evidence is gathering to suggest that there is help at hand for these unfortunate people whose confidence, jobs and even health may be at risk. Research is showing that writer's cramp can be tackled through the mechanics of handwriting, and in that perspective new techniques can be taught which bypass the muscles that are causing the trouble. Our own view is that in most cases the trouble has arisen because of a combination of quite simple factors. Many writer's cramp victims are high achievers and perfectionists as well. However, they often have poor writing posture or strategies that put a considerable amount of strain on their hands, arms or other parts of their bodies. This situation is made worse when the writer is confronted by the extra strain of examinations or perhaps a new job. Then the tension can turn to pain. At that moment the defensive mechanism of the body comes into action and stops the hand from harming itself further. This situation can be defused once the writer understands the cause. A new penhold, such as the one on pages 35 and 36, a more relaxed attitude that takes into account that no one can produce perfect letters at speed, and above all the relief from understanding that they are not suffering from an incurable neurological complaint, all work wonders. With this understanding sufferers can experiment to find better strategies. The alternative penhold alone sorts out many people's problems. However, the worries that have made their lives so difficult may take longer to go away. Gradually the writers relax, and as they relax so it all becomes easier to forget about the worries. Forgetting is most important. As everything became so problematic for those with writer's cramp they began thinking too much about the act of writing. It may sound odd, but in order to recover they need to forget about what they are doing and let the act of writing become automatic again.

One final word of warning. In the case of writer's cramp it is not necessarily a good idea to switch to the other hand. Eventually the second one usually gives up for exactly the same reasons that the natural one did – tension and pain. With the second hand the problems usually arise more rapidly. The worries are by then more acute, and the postural problems may also be worse.

Part two

How to put things right

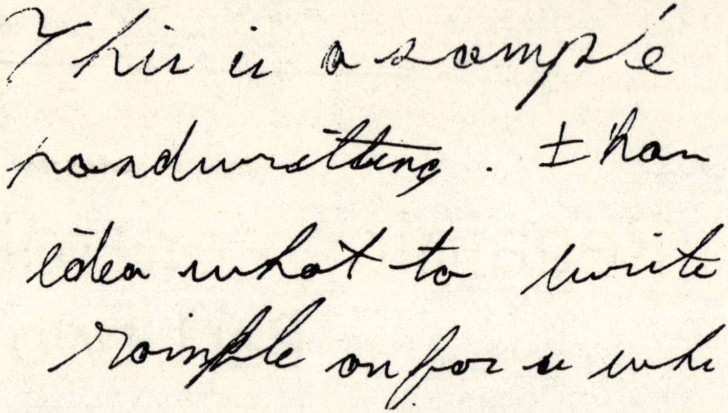

This is a really disorganized handwriting. It is not hand control that is lacking, but a clear idea of what letters should look like. The writer really needs to look on the exercises as a course and work through them from start to finish.

6

Regaining control

Retraining a habit

As you already know, writing movement is a habit. Writing exercises are the best way to begin to retrain that habit. What they *really* train is your brain. You can reprogramme your reactions, and the easiest way is by repetition of pattern: it is the automatic part of your brain that controls your handwriting. When you are writing, you need to be able to forget how to produce the individual letters. Then your mind is free to concentrate on what you are saying, and perhaps your spelling too.

First you must take steps to get rid of any faults. Then you can go on to benefit from the next stages of development. It need not be dull. Rather, it should be satisfying to see how quickly you improve. But work slowly at first: it is important to get things right. You must train a correct movement, not reinforce a wrong one, so do not be tempted to hurry. That is a wasted effort. One good line of pattern is far more valuable than a whole page of badness. There will be plenty of opportunity to speed things up later on.

Skill training is always demanding. This is what handwriting is: a skill. It is the same in the early stages whether you are learning to wrestle or play the violin. First you train and then you practise. In the end it is your automatic responses that control the result.

The exercises which follow can be used as a course, or you can pick out those that you need most. It depends on what you want to change.

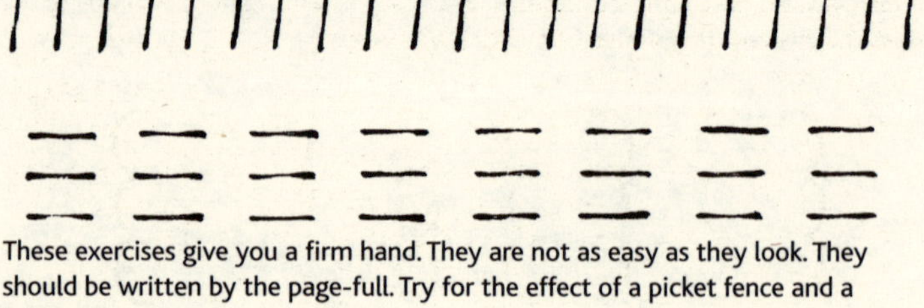

These exercises give you a firm hand. They are not as easy as they look. They should be written by the page-full. Try for the effect of a picket fence and a brick wall.

The first exercises

The first exercises train your hand and eye to work together. You know what it feels like when you want your hand to do something and it does something else instead. These exercises will help you to gain control over your pen.

If your letters are uneven and sprawl all over the place, the early exercises will help you to straighten them up. The exercises may appear childish to you, but please do them all the same. It is important to start with foolproof movements: it will pay off in the end.

The first exercise to practise is just downstrokes, all the same height. They should have the same slant. You may well ask what slant you should choose, if your writing is at different angles. Just do the exercises slowly. After a while you will notice that there is a kind of gentle rhythm that comes naturally to your hand. Your wrist joint and your fingers have their own favourite movement. Find it: that is *your* natural angle. It may slant forward or it may even slant a little backwards. It may be upright. It is nothing to worry about at this stage. The angle may even change a bit as you progress, but the idea is to be consistent.

Then try the other exercises below. You will find some easier than others. What you are doing is practising the basic strokes that make up parts of letters.

These exercises have basic letterforms. They teach you movement. Feel free to break the line and lift your hand whenever you wish.

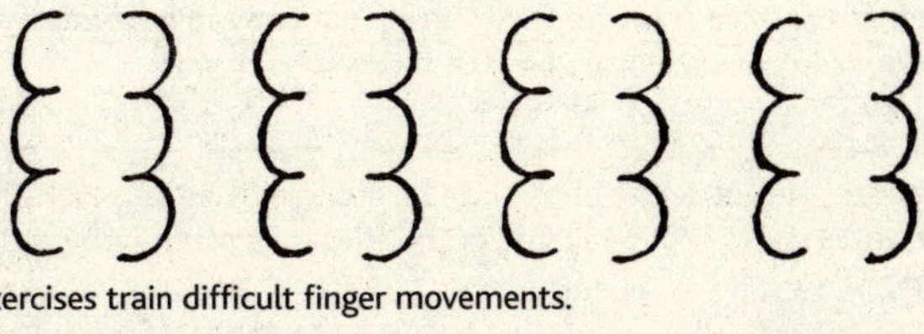

These exercises train difficult finger movements.

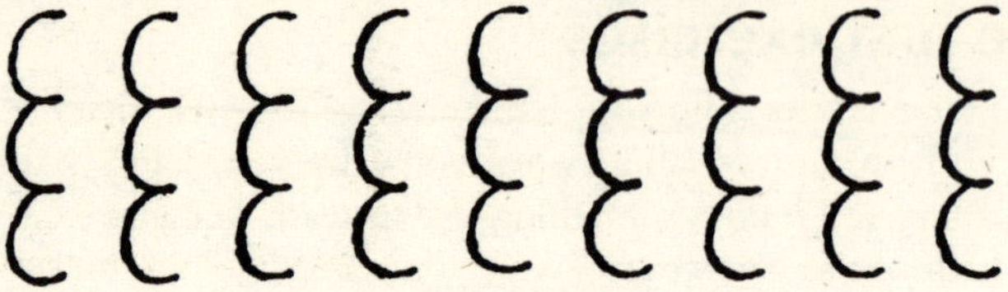

You should be able to write a full page of these in five or ten minutes.

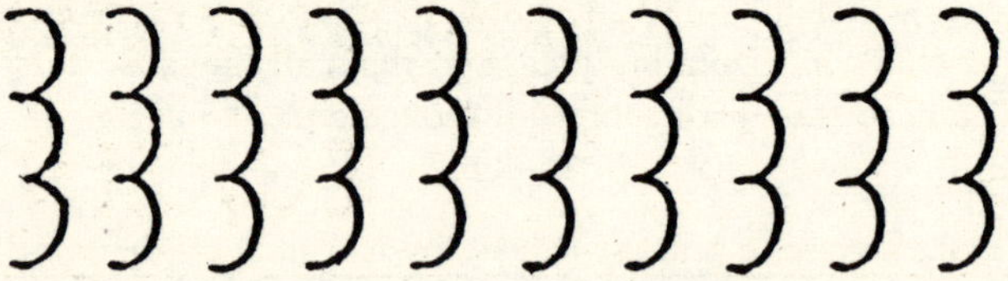

Make sure that, when you get to the bottom line, you are taking as much care as you did at the beginning.

WHAT IF THESE EXERCISES ARE GETTING YOU NOWHERE?

In the beginning some people have real difficulty in reproducing the exercises. The answer is to simplify them until your hand is ready to do what you want it to.

You can trace over the printed exercises. That may help. There is an even easier way. You can make up your own scribble and trace over that. It is quite a different approach. The reason that it is easy for you is that you are tracing over a line that is your own natural movement.

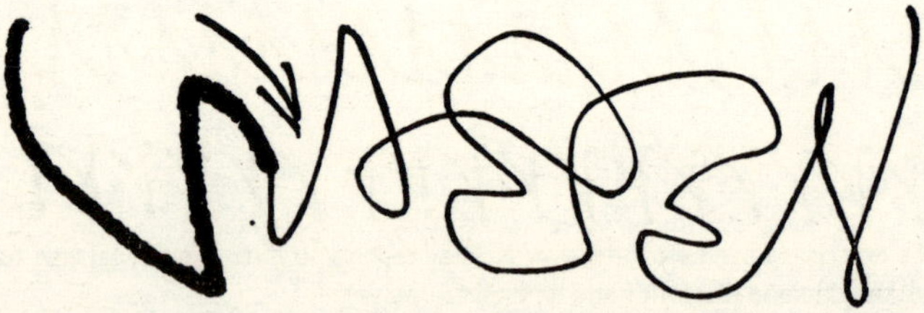

This is your last resort. If you have trouble even tracing the exercises, try tracing a scribble that you have drawn yourself. You are not likely to have much difficulty tracing over your own movement, because it is natural to you.

7

Rhythm and texture

Before you start working on individual letters it is a good idea to think about what writing really is.

Writing is a pattern of certain strokes that make recognizable letters. A pattern of letters makes up a word. Letters can be written separately. They can be joined up – or even simply suggested, as they sometimes are in a fast cursive.

Good handwriting has a rhythm of its own. An even texture improves appearance and helps legibility. You will probably have developed your personal rhythm in spite of what you were taught about the shape or style of letters. This is your own personality showing through. Your rhythm can change. Perhaps you have noticed how you write differently when you are tired or in a hurry. A new pen can make a difference too.

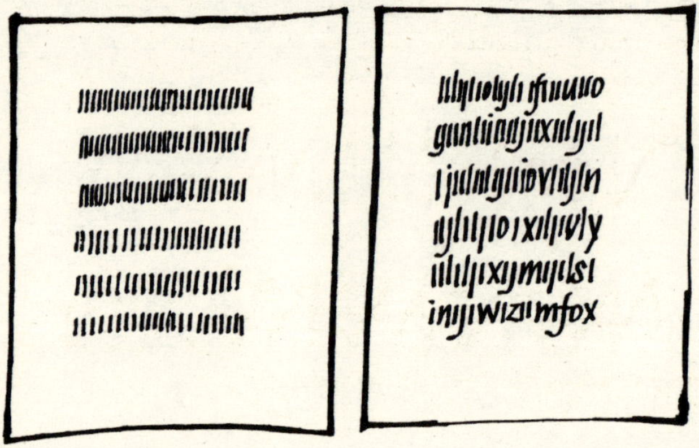

Writing is just a pattern of strokes. The sheet on the left has meaningless strokes. On the right some patterns have recognition points that make them into letters.

You do not need many recognition points to read a scribble. You may sacrifice some points for speed, but you need the general silhouette of the word, especially the beginning and the end.

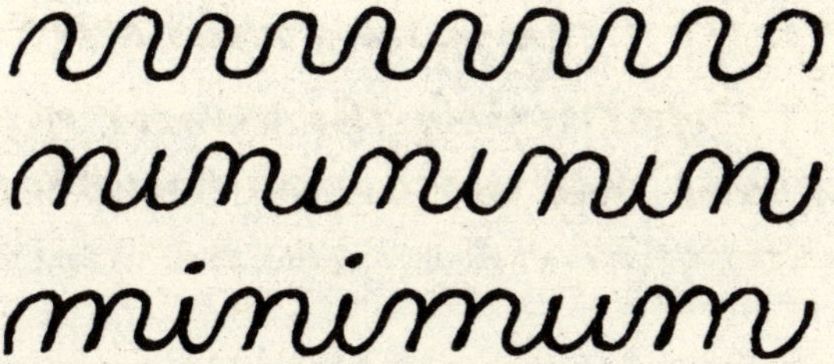

By nature, people have different movement patterns.

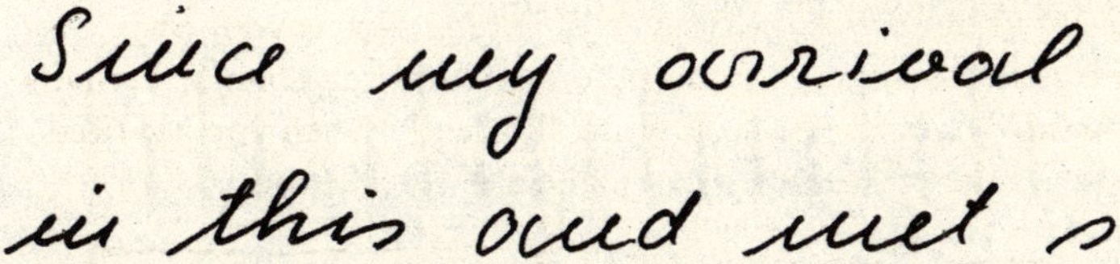

This sample of writing is naturally rounded.

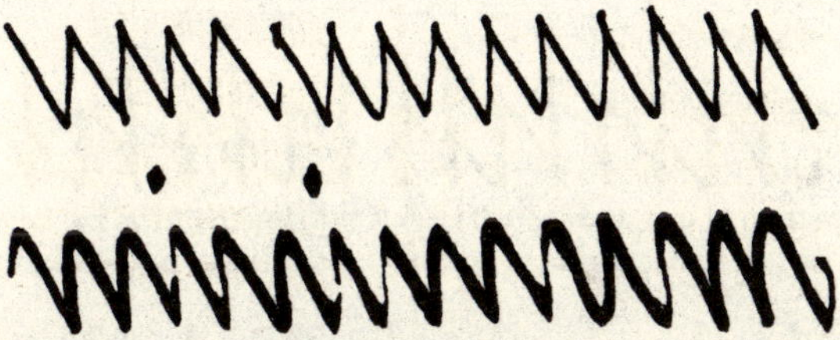

Some people's writing is inclined to slope backwards.

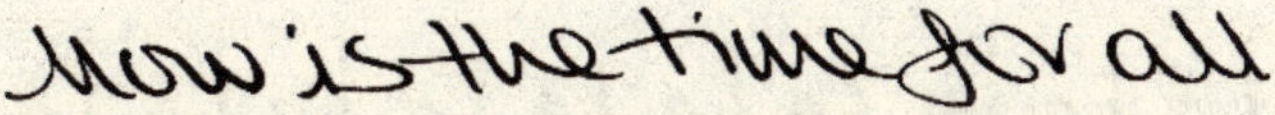

This left-hander has a speedy and attractive backward-sloping hand.

A pointed hand comes naturally to many people.

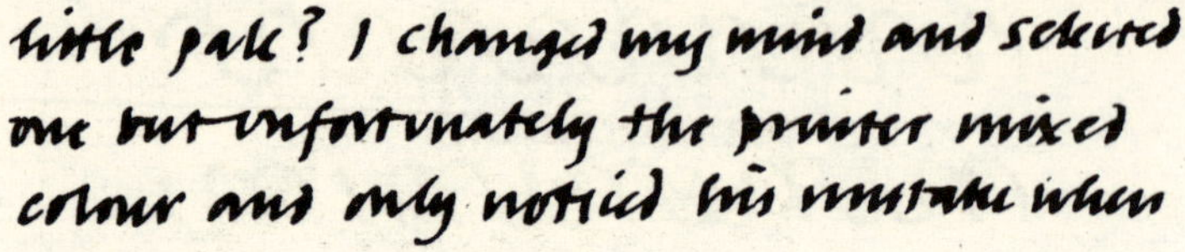

If this precise hand did not have frequent recognition points, it might be difficult to read.

In most cases it is fairly easy to pick out the overall rhythm and pattern of a hand. Look at the patterns illustrated and see which one most closely fits your handwriting.

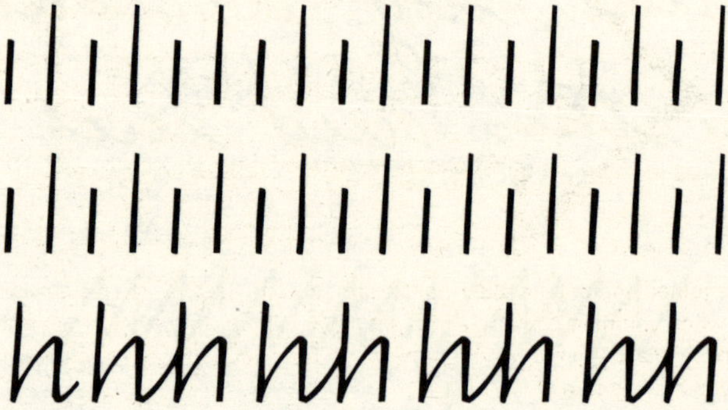

A regular pattern of long and short strokes is the skeleton for many important letters. Closely related letters such as **h** and **b** share the same lines and arches.

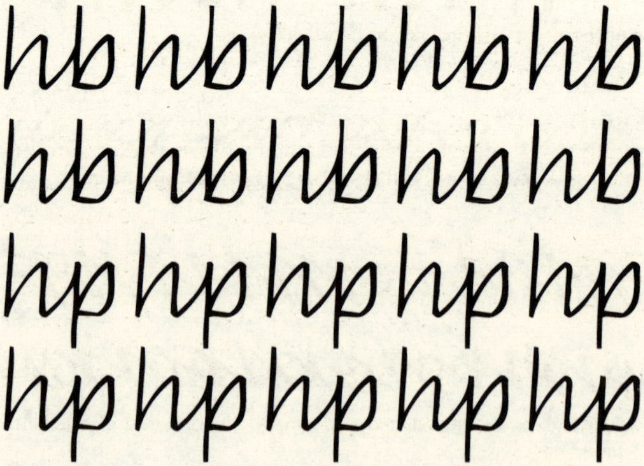

At the bottom of the page substitute the letter **p** for **b** where shown.

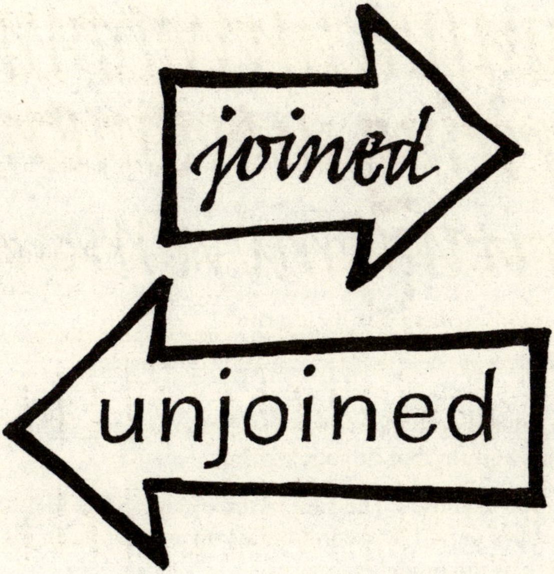

You use joined and unjoined letters for different purposes. Joined letters are better when you have to write a lot. When you join up correctly formed letters, they give you a rhythmic writing movement. Then your writing is legible even when you are in a hurry.

First of all, try these exercises in your usual way, with your usual slant and familiar pen. Do them slowly and carefully, otherwise they will not be much use.

Do not throw away your trial work. Keep it all, however bad it looks. Glance through it from time to time to see how you are changing and improving. These same exercises will benefit you again when you are retraining yourself with the help of the model.

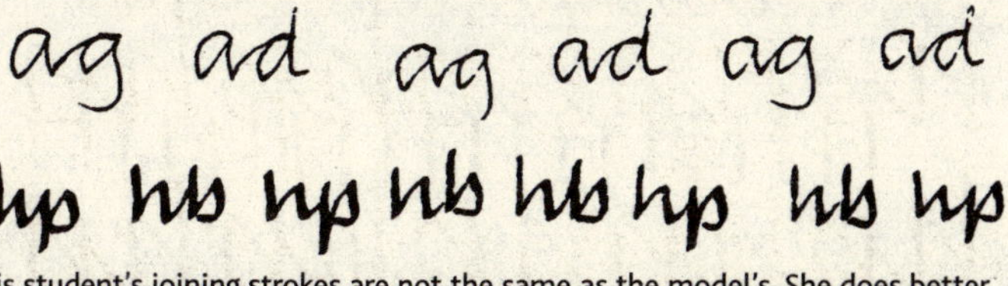

This student's joining strokes are not the same as the model's. She does better with a broad-edge nib.

Writing is a movement pattern with enough recognition points to make it legible. Notice how little you have to add to a zig-zag to make words.

The way the underlying strokes are formed clearly influences the final slant and rhythm of your writing.

Look at the exercises. They are in three stages. The first has the downstrokes only. The second builds up a skeleton. In the third, the letters of the model emerge.

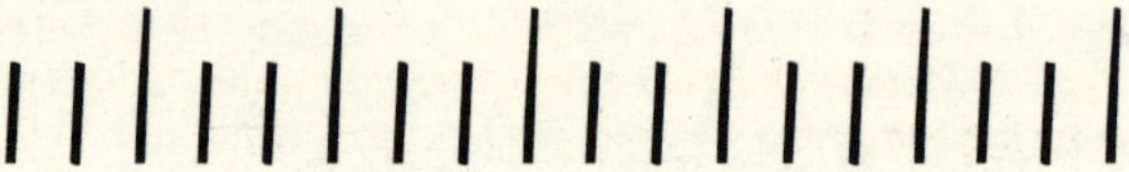

The first line shows you the basic movement that you need to master.

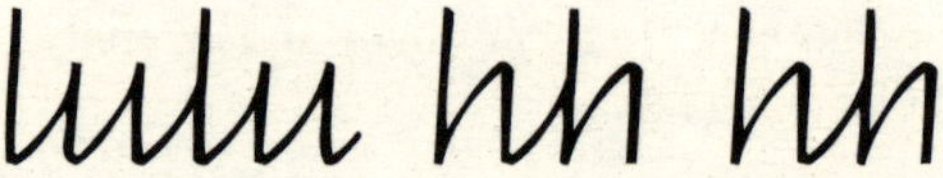

The second teaches you movement – how to join the downstrokes.

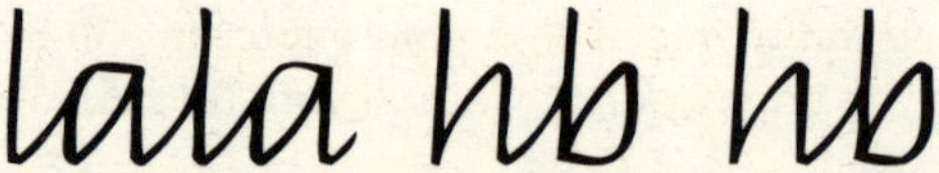

In the third you see the fully formed letters emerging from the pattern.

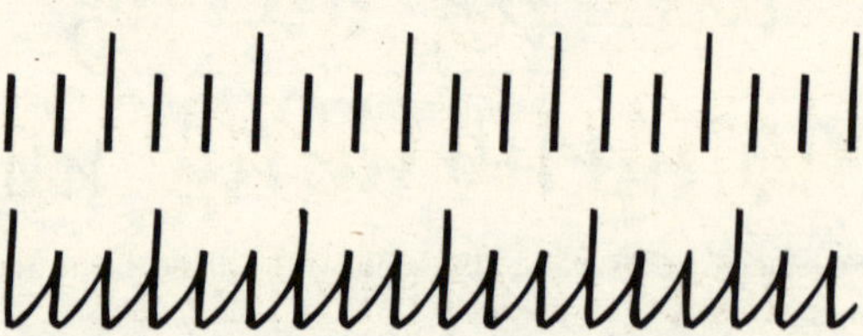

A simple exercise of small letters and ascending ones is a good place to start controlling your letterforms. Try to get as even a pattern as possible.

This exercise teaches you the movement pattern of the **u** arch.

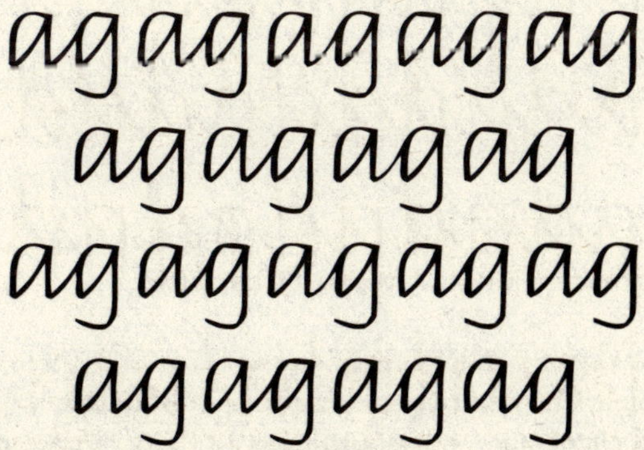

With small modifications you end up with **a** and **g**.

You should come back and try the exercises again later on, and compare the results.

What stops so many people from improving their handwriting is a fixed image in their mind of what a letter should be. Take the letter **a**. Most people would describe it as a roundish character or perhaps an **o** with a tail. The exercises show that an **a** can equally well be thought of as two parallel vertical lines. When writing these lines, the pen is kept on the paper as it travels from the bottom of the first line to the top of the second. The flat introductory stroke shown at the third stage makes this pattern of lines into a recognizable letter **a**.

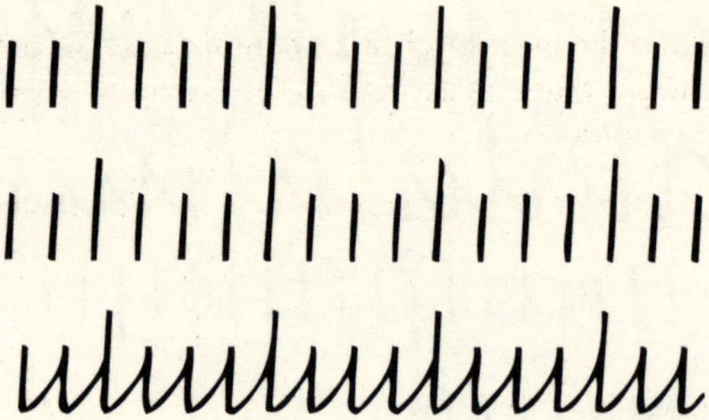

This exercise has the same starting point as the one on the previous page.

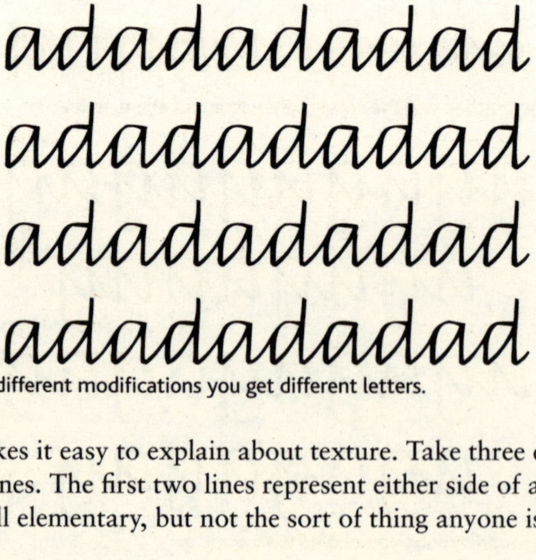

By adding different modifications you get different letters.

This makes it easy to explain about texture. Take three evenly spaced lines. The first two lines represent either side of a letter. This is all elementary, but not the sort of thing anyone is ever taught at school. It is up to you how close or at what angle these basic lines are written. Your personal texture and rhythm is the result.

A *consistent* rhythm and texture is one of the most important marks of a good handwriting.

There is nothing magical about writing. A certain shape has come to represent a certain sound in English. In French, for example, which also uses the Latin alphabet, the same letter may be pronounced differently. Then there are languages such as Greek or Russian that use different alphabets. Here the same shape may represent a totally different letter.

Learning to write means learning to put these stroke patterns into a sequence that you and others can then read back. *The purpose of writing is to communicate.*

8

A training model

This alphabet is solely a training model. It is based on movement pattern, a good starting point for development. It is a sturdy style with healthy mechanics. You are meant to learn it and then leave it. It does not matter whether your natural hand is rounder or narrower, more upright or slanting. After you have used the model to retrain, you can go back to a more personal way of writing. Your movement, rhythm and style will by then be much improved.

When you first look at these letters, you may not like them at all. They may not look in the least like your own handwriting. They may not be your idea of good writing, much less what you want yours to develop into.

The angular shapes may be somewhat unfamiliar. However, they have a special job to do in retraining. The distinctive flat top of the letters **a**, **d**, **g** and **q** has a definite purpose. You cannot ignore the essential first stroke that results in a closed-up letter. If you leave your **a**'s and g's open, as many people do, they get confused with **u** and **y**.

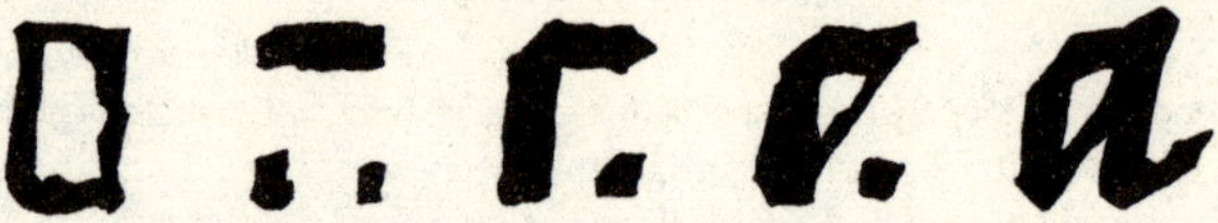

The Italian writing master Ludovico Arrighi published a very influential handwriting manual dated 1522. This illustration shows his method for teaching basic letterforms. Please note the flat top and the triangular shape of the letter. It is our starting point.

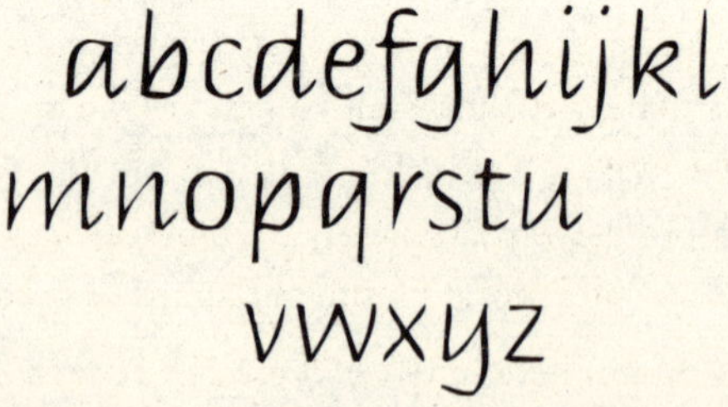

A model alphabet should be strong enough for you to lean on, practical enough to fill your weeks while you are using it, and impersonal enough to be easily discarded.

abcdefgh
ijklmno
pqrstu
vwxyz

This model has a slightly unusual shape. It is meant to ensure that you learn a correct movement.

Now look at the stroke that springs up from the bottom of those same letters. It saves time, makes a clearer letter, and then encourages a straight downstroke. Notice that it is not a sharp corner but a subtly rounded one.

The value of the model is in training the right movement. Good habits remain. They will still show when you go on to develop a more personal style.

In case you find it hard to adjust to a few of the letters, there are alternatives. The habits of a lifetime are hard to break.

The model is shown here in three sizes. The reason is that different people write in different sizes which vary enormously. You will probably relate to the one nearest your own writing, but the largest one may be best to trace. Try all three and see which suits you.

abcd

efghijkl

mnopqrstu

vwxyz

The model is presented in three different sizes for a very good reason. Research has shown that different people relate to different sizes.

WHY THIS ALPHABET SHOULD NOT BE USED FOR CHILDREN

There is a great deal of difference between retraining adults and teaching young children. *This alphabet should not be used for teaching children*. It is specially designed for adults who can understand the reasons for its structure. They will use it as it is meant to be used, as an intermediate training aid.

Children might well simplify the stages in an attempt to copy them. Then they will risk ending up with too angular a way of writing at an early, impressionable age.

v w y y

v w y y

Some people write rounded letters while others prefer pointed ones. The alphabet is flexible and allows you a wide choice. Just look at the different v's, w's and y's in these samples.

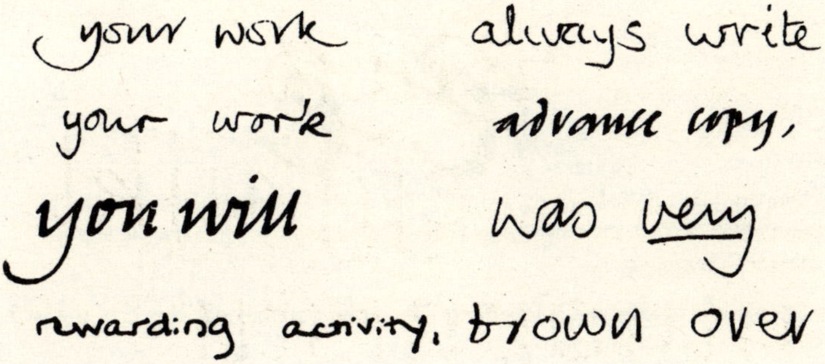

Alternatives

Some letters in the model will be quite different from the ones that you were taught or that you are using now. Some have been designed with a special purpose in mind. It will profit you to follow them closely. There are perfectly good alternatives for other letters.

The letters **v** and **w** can equally well be round or pointed. You do not want to change anything unnecessarily. Both forms are shown, for you to choose which you like better. There are other ways of writing **y** and **x** too.

The model has two e's. One is a simple loop. The other is written in two strokes. If you feel you cannot change the way you have written since schooldays, then do not worry: carry on with the familiar one-stroke letter. It is worth experimenting, though. The two-stroke letter is not only attractive but joins more easily in some letter combinations.

In the model, the basic form of the letters **s** and **f** is used. This is to reinforce the correct writing movement. These two letters change considerably when joined up and written fast. They also change according to whether they come at the beginning of a word, the middle or the end. You will probably have developed your own forms, whatever way you were taught at school.

Alternative forms of **f** and **s** come later, in the chapter on personal modifications. Joined-up double letters that can be learned as a single symbol are shown there too.

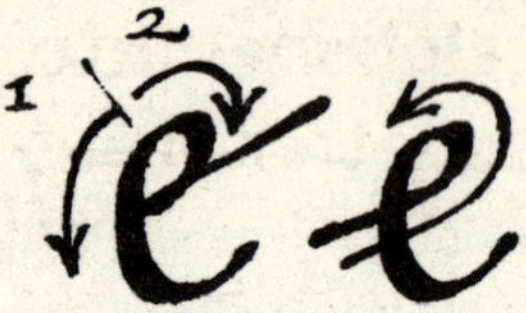

There are two ways of writing a small **e**. For centuries people used to write it in two strokes. In fact the looped one only became popular when people started using a pointed pen.

Although the looped one is much more common, you may discover that the two-stroke one has advantages.

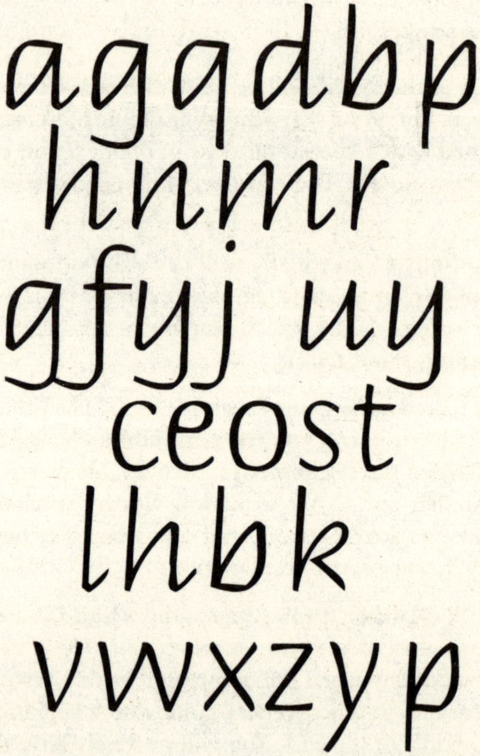

There are families of letters that have the same shapes. You will gain from practising those letters that are related to each other. Then you are repeating the same shapes over and over again.

g shares the loop with some letters, and a descending stroke with others.

Dividing the alphabet into stroke-related letter groups

You almost certainly think of letters in alphabetical order. It is very difficult *not* to start with **a, b, c.**

These exercises are different. You divide the letters into stroke-related groups. Then you write and repeat the same shapes. You compare letters that have similar strokes, and watch them change and improve together as the exercises progress.

You learn more quickly this way. Letters in alphabetical order have all the strokes mixed. In the early stages that would make life unnecessarily difficult.

1234567890

1234567890

? : ; , ; , “-”—!

These numerals came into use much later than our small letters. Their shapes are much closer to the shapes of capital letters. They do not join up.

Numerals can either be all the same height, like capital letters, or they can ascend and descend.

ɒ ɒɒɒ bmnphrk

ɑ ɑɑɑ adgquy

o oooo ceo

v www vw yxz

These exercises teach you the basic shapes of the letters in the different families. Before you write the letters, do a few lines of each basic shape. Try to think of them as patterns only, until you start adding the strokes that turn them into letters.

Exercises for each group of letters

There is a special exercise for most groups of letters. Each exercise teaches the shapes and movements that you need. It is *easier* to master them in pattern than in writing.

The first two are unusual but efficient. They train you in the springy arches that are a feature of the model.

Try each pattern separately until you can do it well. Then write the family of letters that the pattern applies to. This leads naturally on to handwriting. The real problems arise when you mix the different letter families as you do in writing any ordinary word. Approach this in the same way, through pattern.

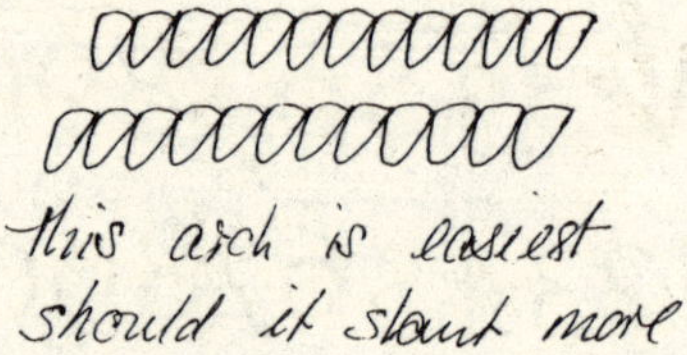

Some students find one arch easier, some another.

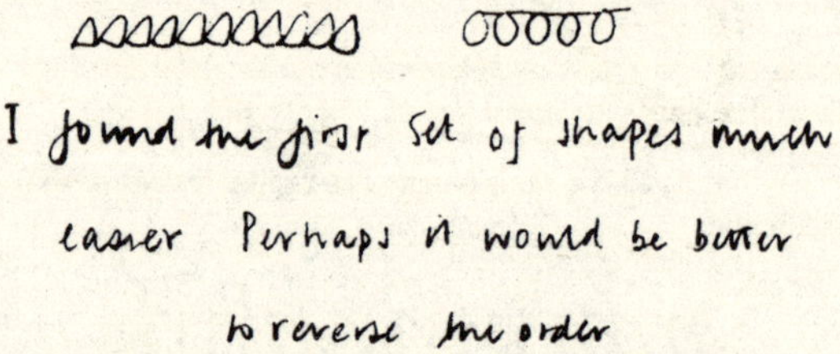

These examples also show the different sizes that people choose to work in.

Others just think the exercises look like a set of false teeth!

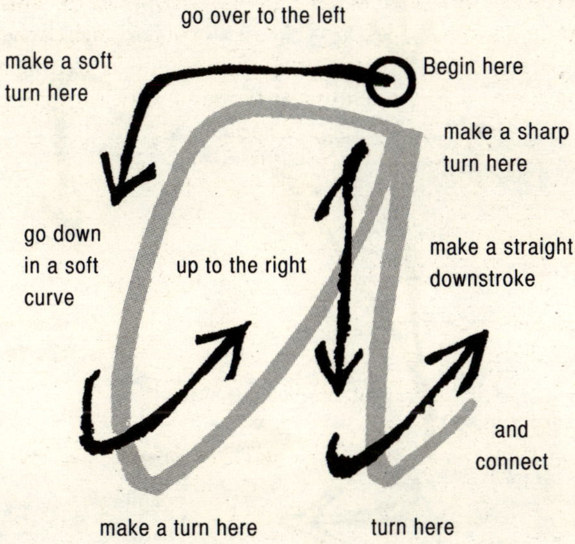
go over to the left
make a soft
turn here
Begin here
make a sharp
turn here
go down
in a soft
curve
up to the right
make a straight
downstroke
and
connect
make a turn here
turn here

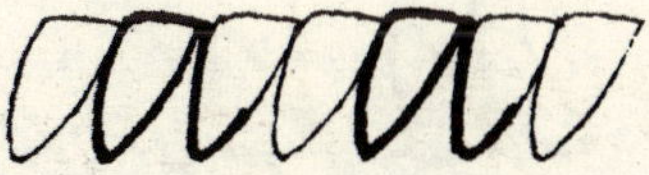

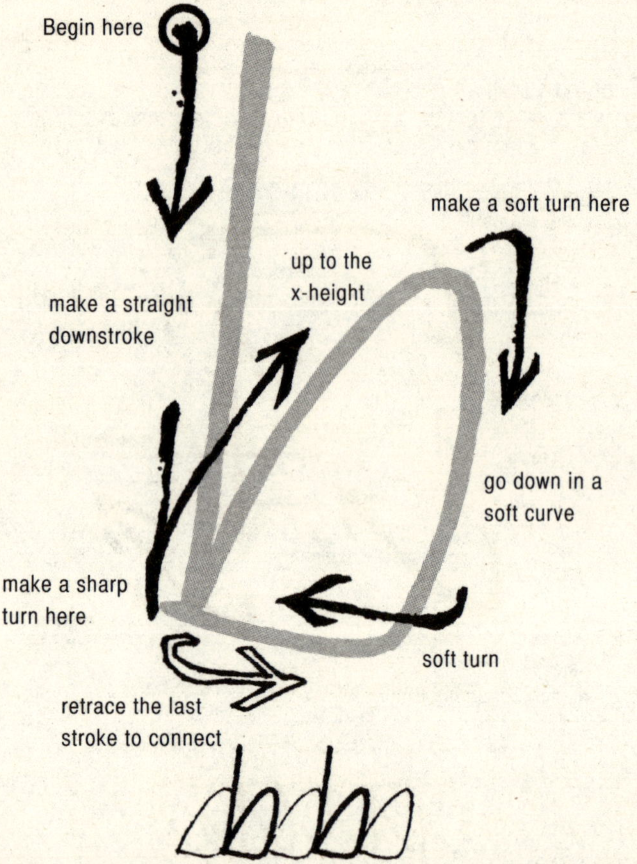

Begin here
make a straight
downstroke
up to the
x-height
make a soft turn here
go down in a
soft curve
make a sharp
turn here
soft turn
retrace the last
stroke to connect

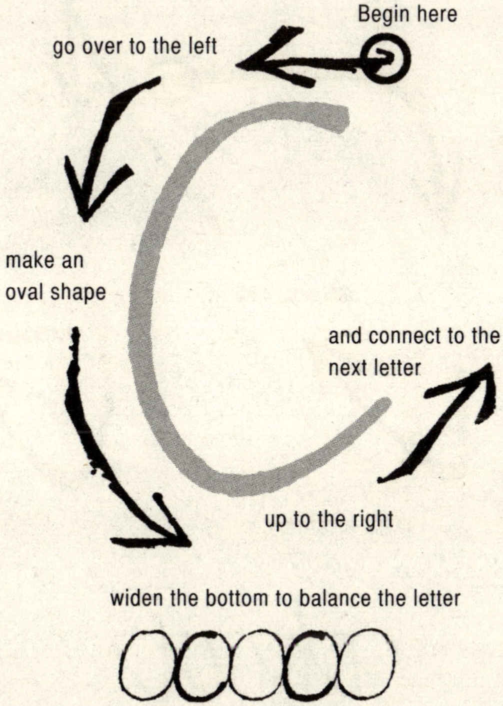
Begin here
go over to the left
make an
oval shape
and connect to the
next letter
up to the right
widen the bottom to balance the letter

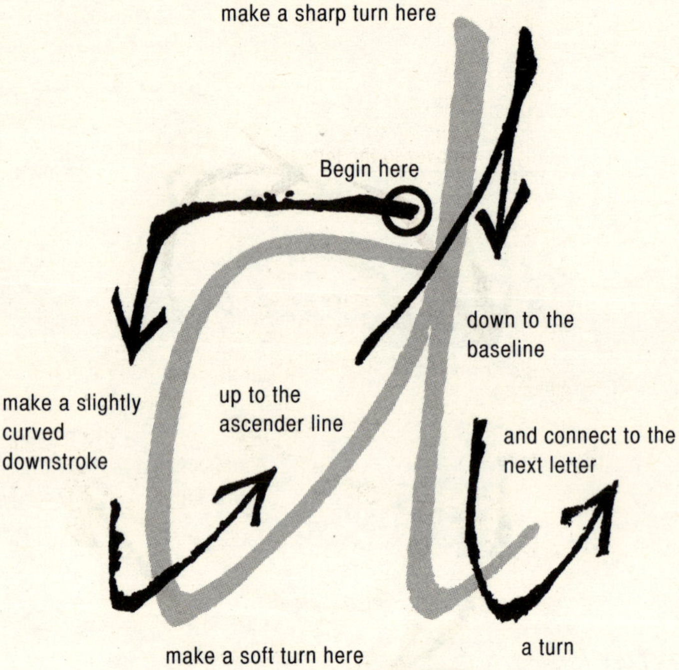
make a sharp turn here
Begin here
down to the
baseline
make a slightly
curved
downstroke
up to the
ascender line
and connect to the
next letter
make a soft turn here
a turn

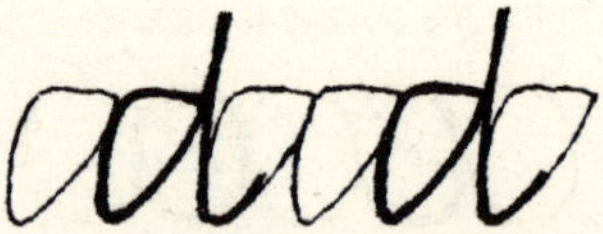

A one-stroke **e**

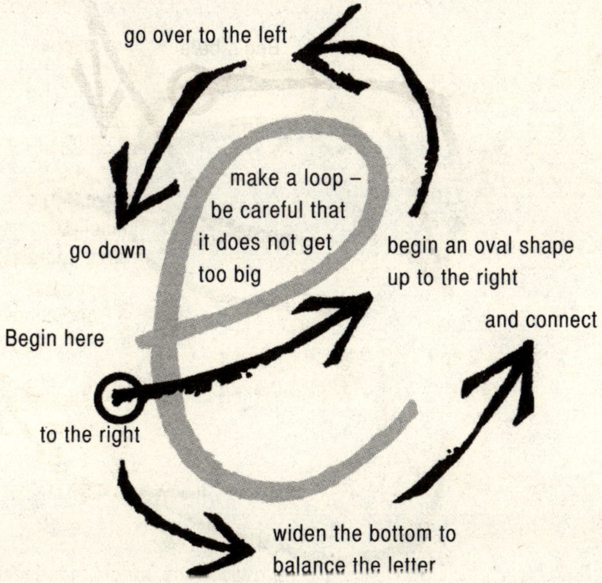

A two-stroke **e**

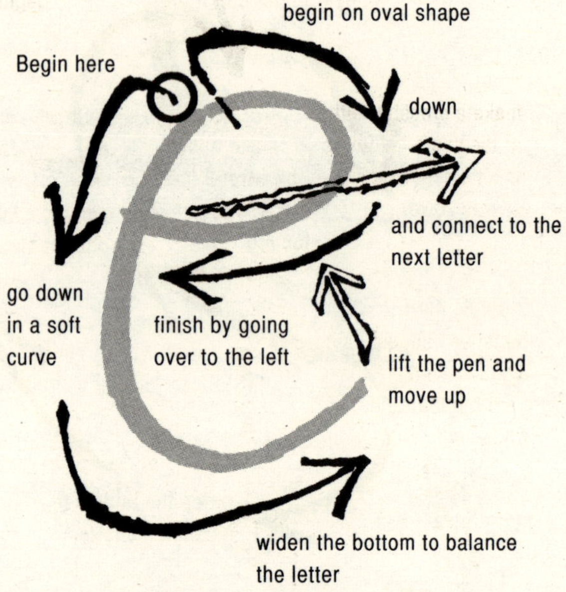

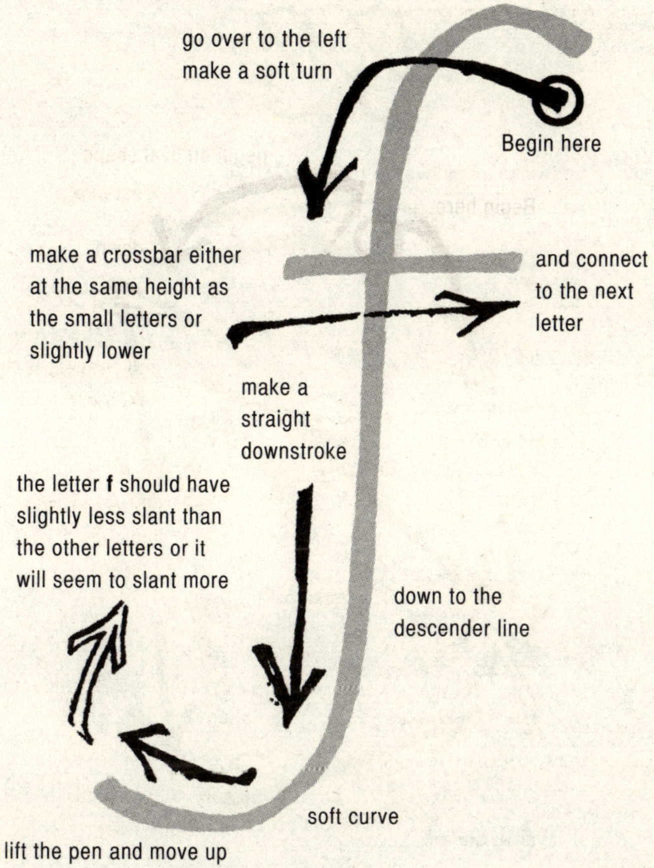
go over to the left
make a soft turn
Begin here
make a crossbar either at the same height as the small letters or slightly lower
and connect to the next letter
make a straight downstroke
the letter f should have slightly less slant than the other letters or it will seem to slant more
down to the descender line
soft curve
lift the pen and move up

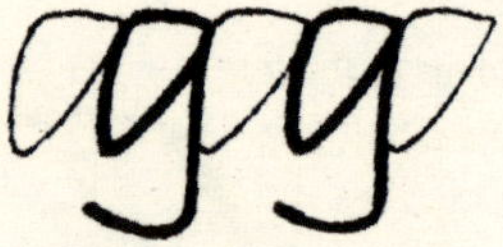

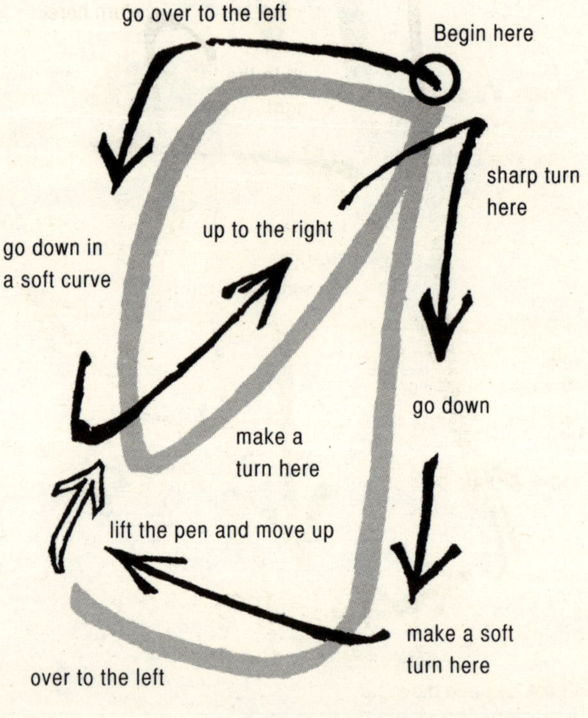
go over to the left
Begin here
sharp turn here
up to the right
go down in a soft curve
go down
make a turn here
lift the pen and move up
make a soft turn here
over to the left

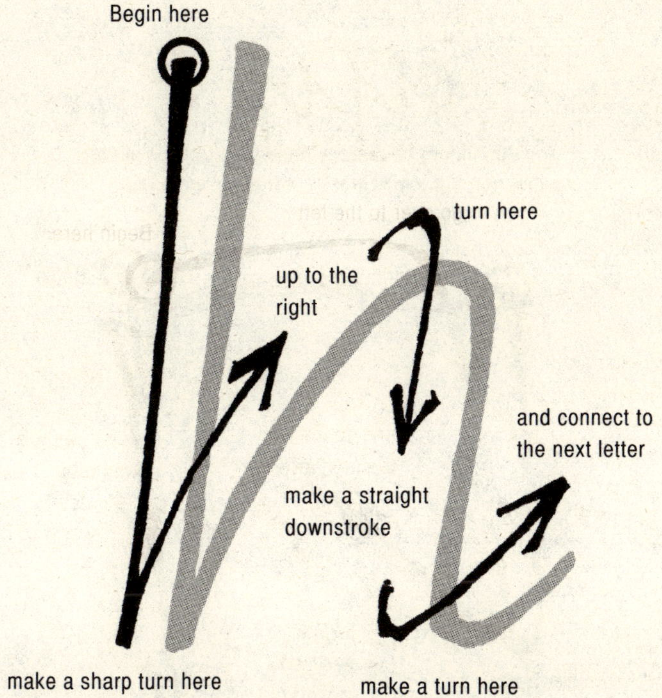
Begin here
turn here
up to the
right
and connect to
the next letter
make a straight
downstroke
make a sharp turn here
make a turn here

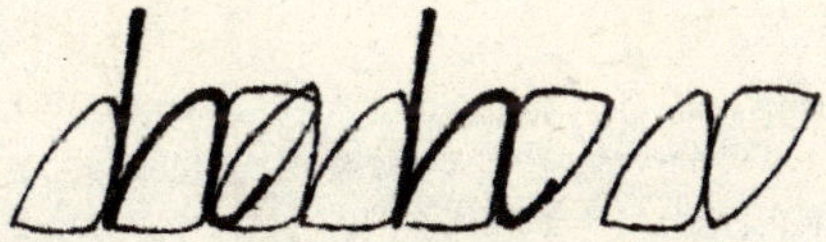

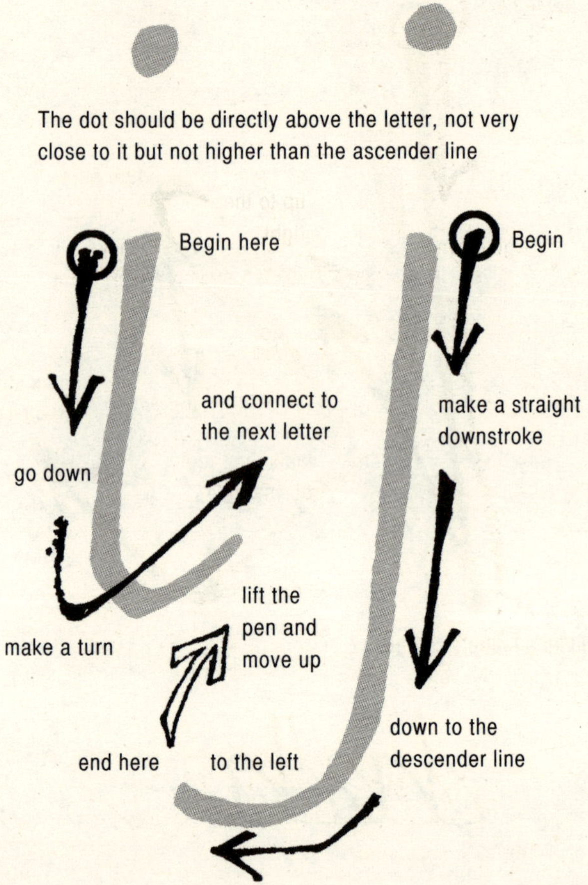
The dot should be directly above the letter, not very close to it but not higher than the ascender line
Begin here
go down
make a turn
and connect to the next letter
Begin
make a straight downstroke
down to the descender line
to the left
lift the pen and move up
end here

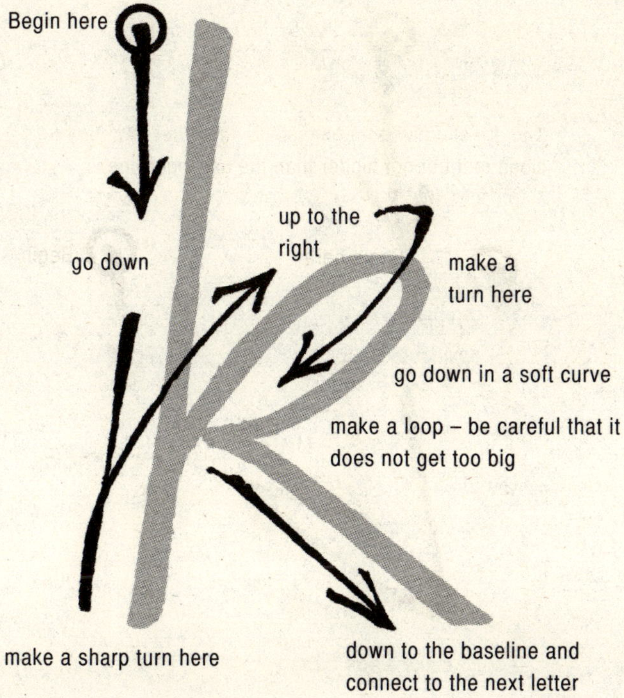
Begin here
go down
up to the
right
make a
turn here
go down in a soft curve
make a loop – be careful that it
does not get too big
make a sharp turn here
down to the baseline and
connect to the next letter

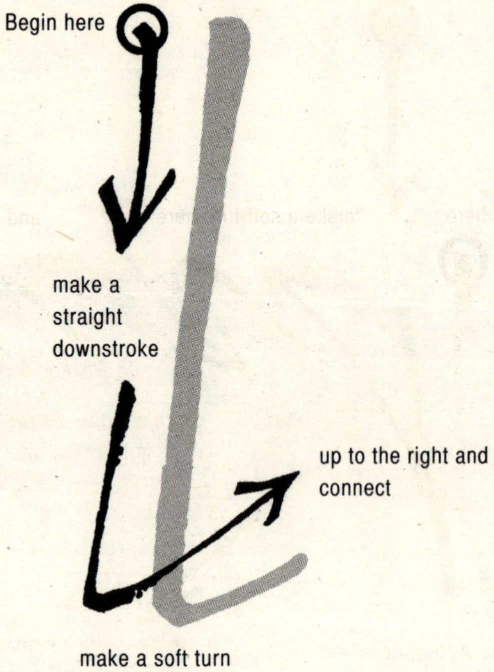
Begin here
make a
straight
downstroke
up to the right and
connect
make a soft turn

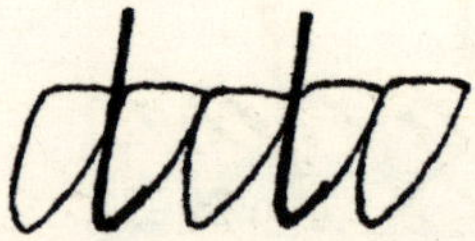

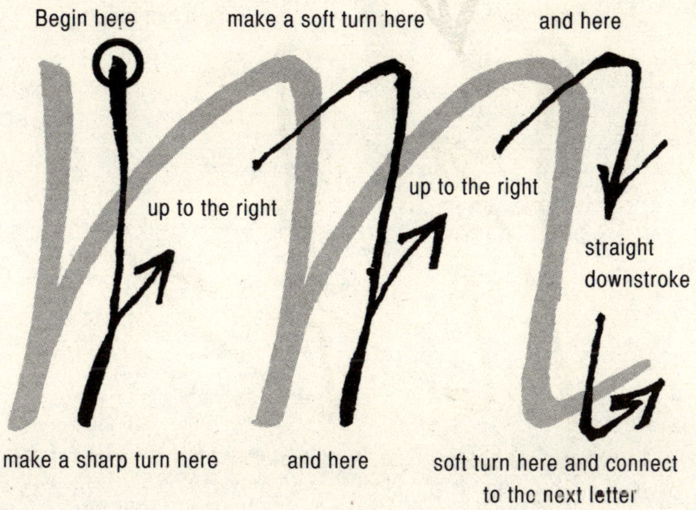
Begin here
make a soft turn here
and here
up to the right
up to the right
straight
downstroke
make a sharp turn here
and here
soft turn here and connect
to the next letter

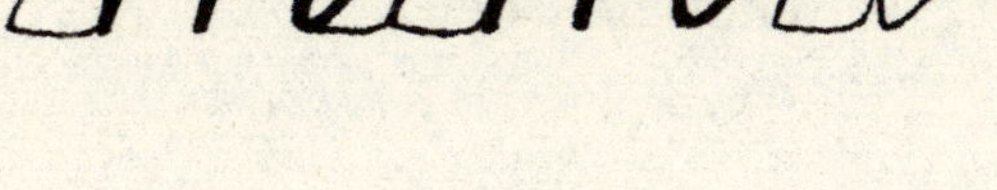

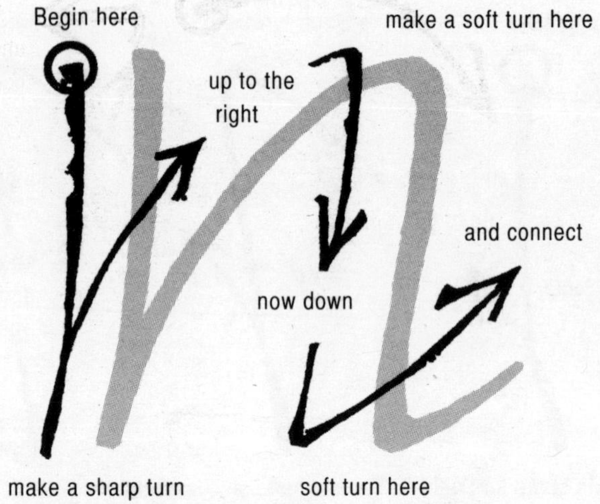
Begin here
make a soft turn here
up to the right
and connect
now down
make a sharp turn
soft turn here

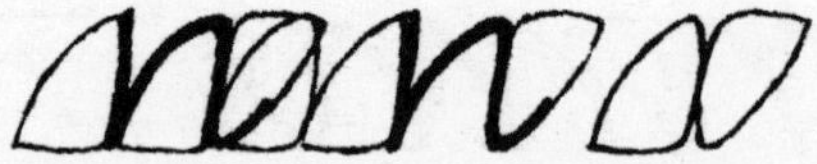

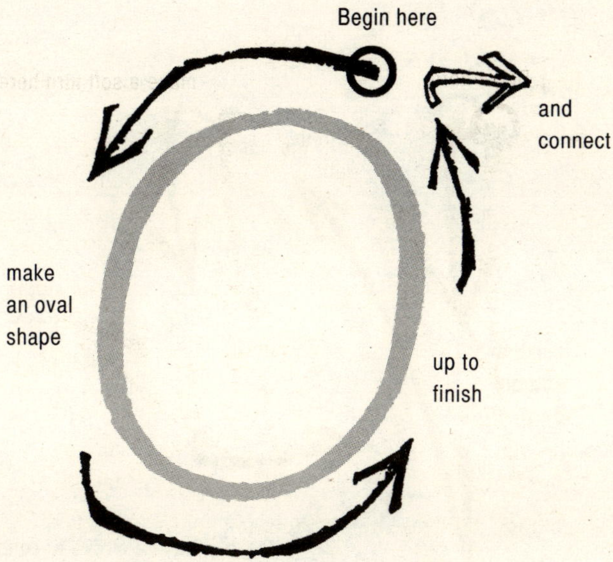
Begin here
and
connect
make
an oval
shape
up to
finish

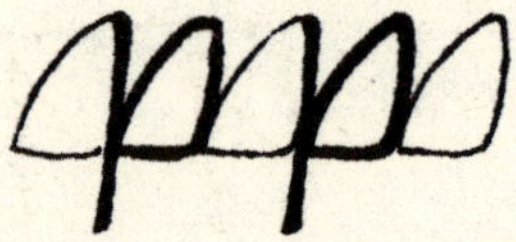

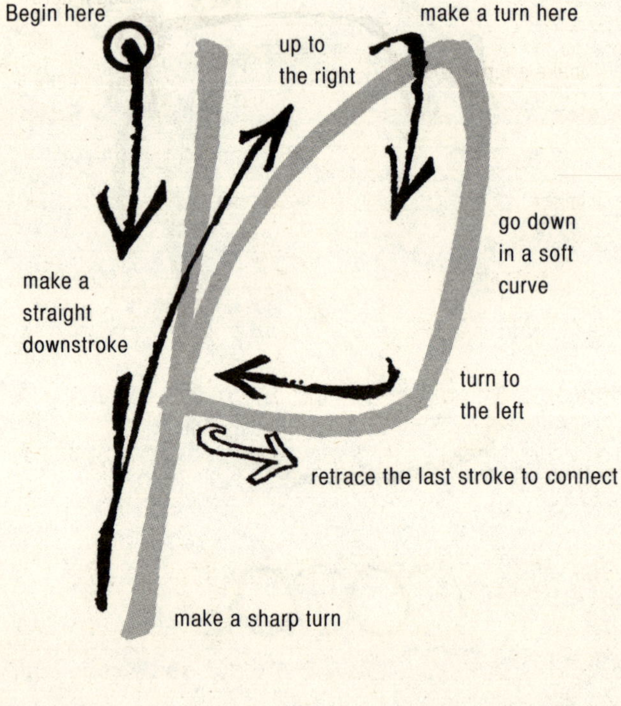
Begin here
up to
the right
make a turn here
go down
in a soft
curve
make a
straight
downstroke
turn to
the left
retrace the last stroke to connect
make a sharp turn

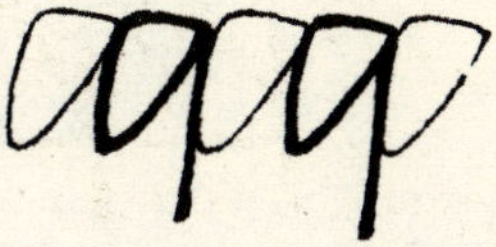

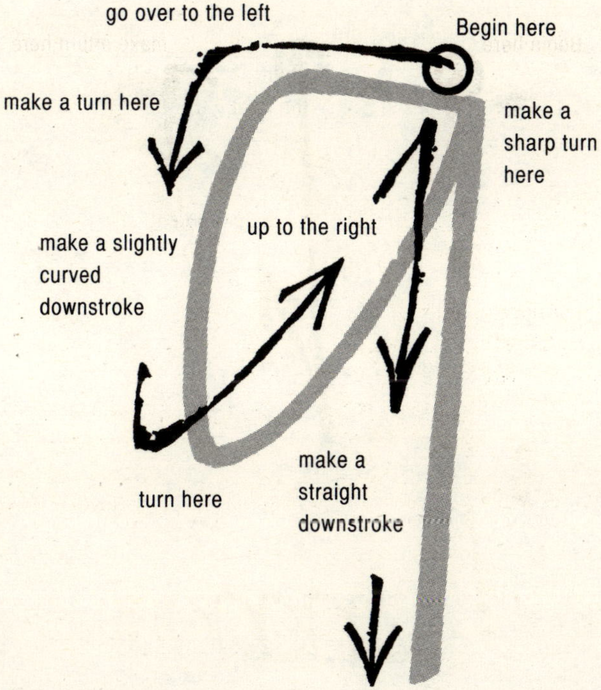
go over to the left
Begin here
make a turn here
make a
sharp turn
here
up to the right
make a slightly
curved
downstroke
turn here
make a
straight
downstroke

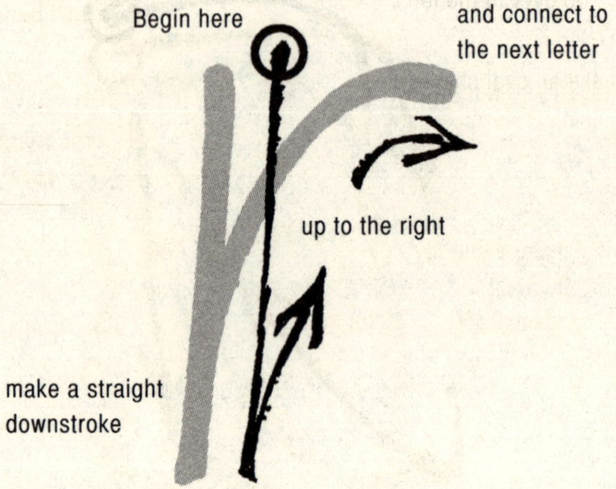
Begin here
and connect to the next letter
up to the right
make a straight downstroke

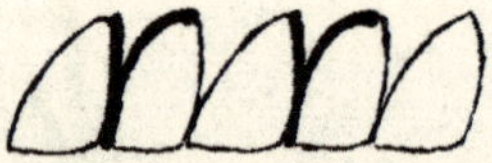

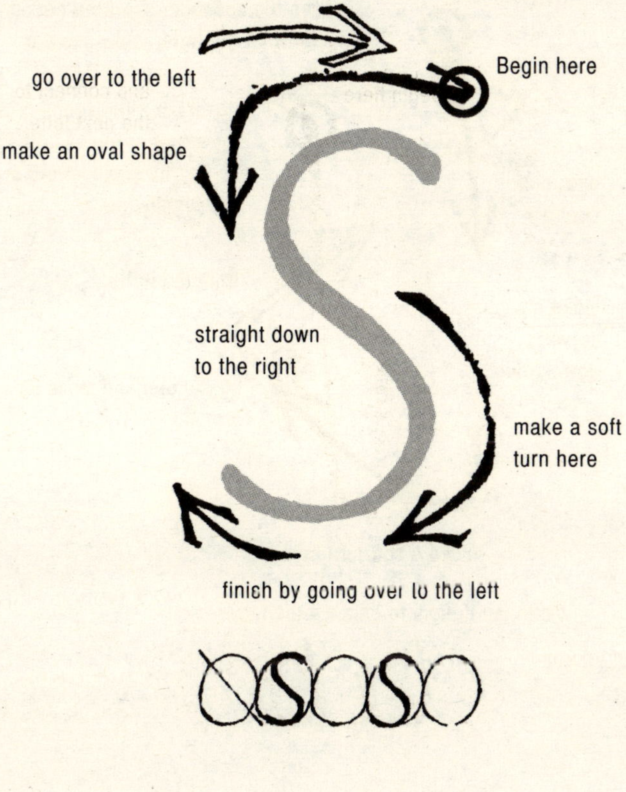

go over to the left
Begin here
make an oval shape
straight down
to the right
make a soft
turn here
finish by going over to the left

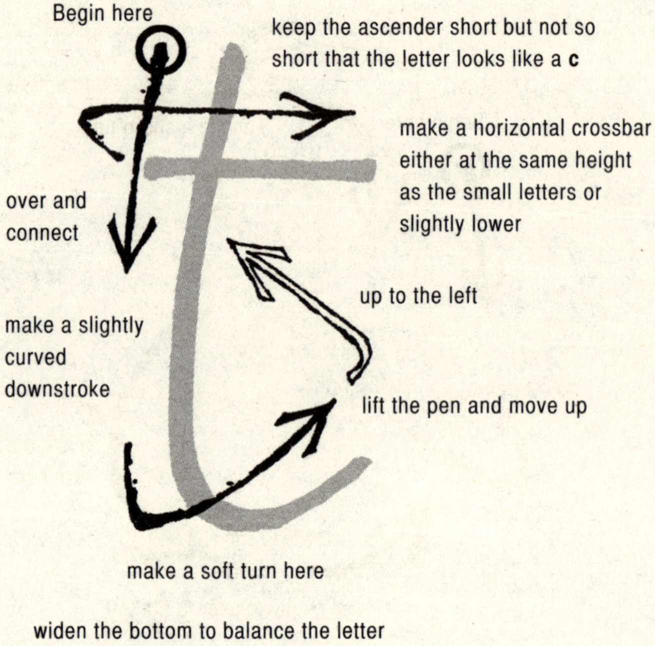
Begin here
keep the ascender short but not so short that the letter looks like a **c**
make a horizontal crossbar either at the same height as the small letters or slightly lower
over and connect
up to the left
make a slightly curved downstroke
lift the pen and move up
make a soft turn here
widen the bottom to balance the letter

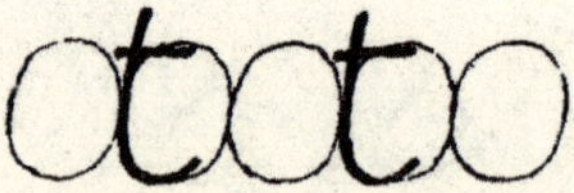

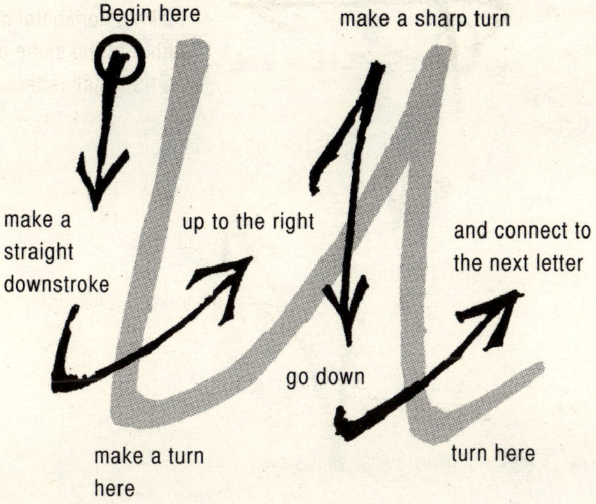
Begin here
make a sharp turn
make a
straight
downstroke
up to the right
and connect to
the next letter
go down
make a turn
here
turn here

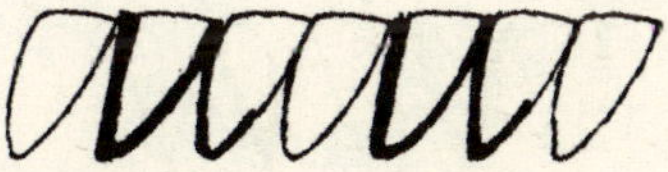

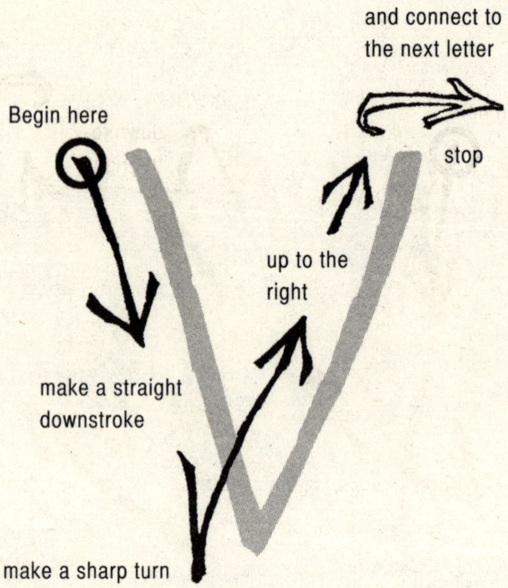
and connect to
the next letter
Begin here
stop
up to the
right
make a straight
downstroke
make a sharp turn

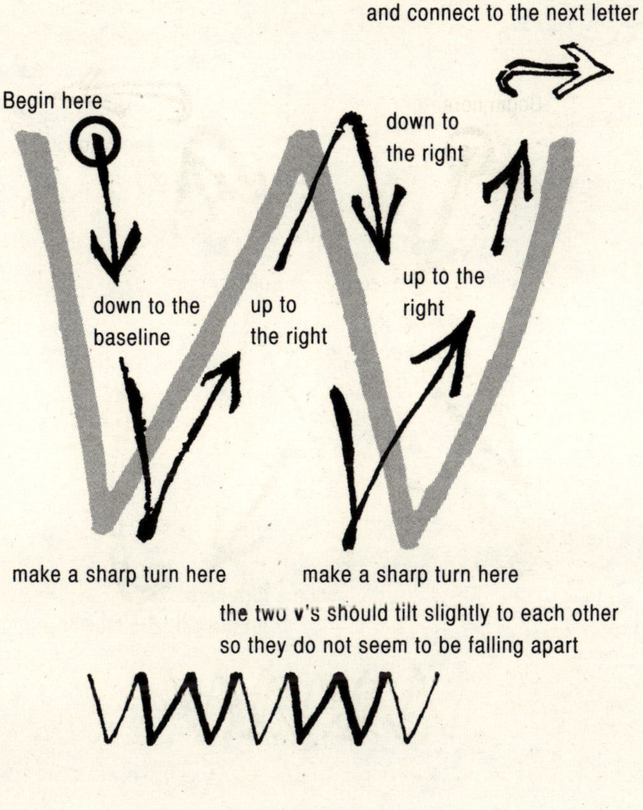
and connect to the next letter
Begin here
down to
the right
up to the
right
down to the
baseline
up to
the right
make a sharp turn here
make a sharp turn here
the two v's should tilt slightly to each other
so they do not seem to be falling apart

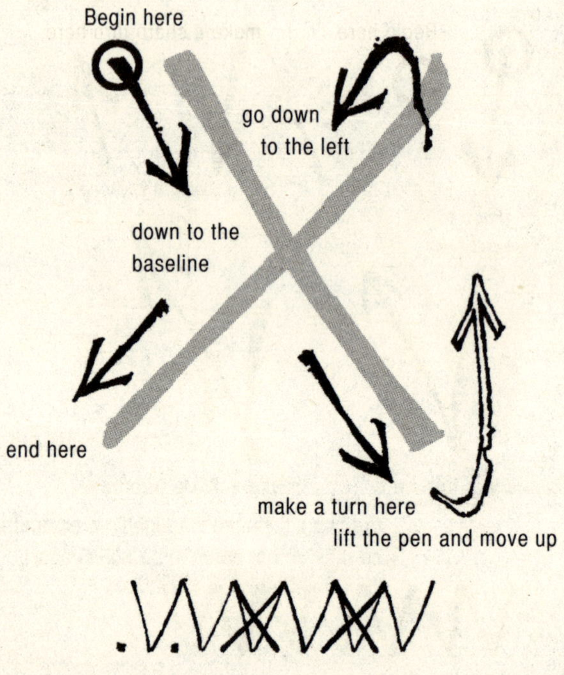
Begin here
go down
to the left
down to the
baseline
end here
make a turn here
lift the pen and move up

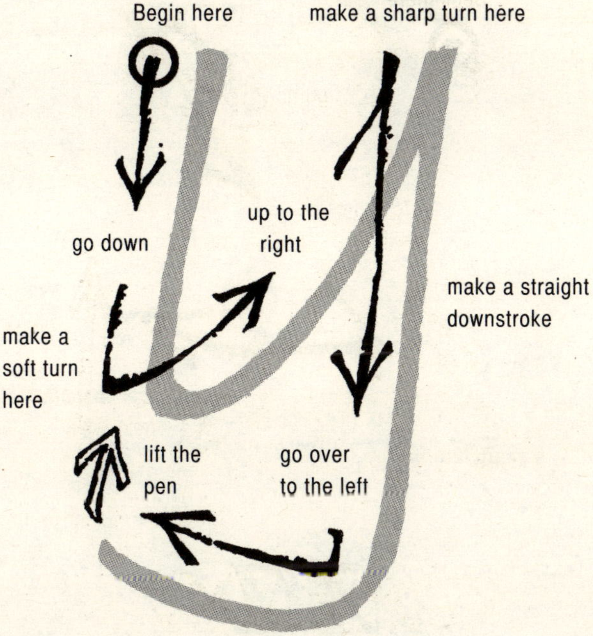
Begin here
make a sharp turn here
go down
up to the right
make a straight downstroke
make a soft turn here
lift the pen
go over to the left

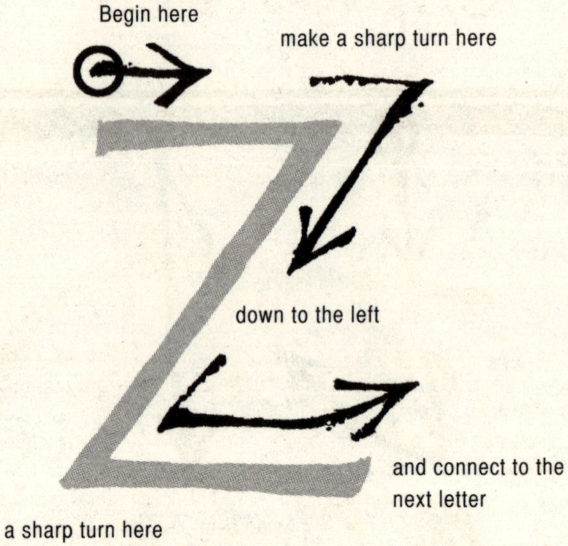
Begin here
make a sharp turn here
down to the left
and connect to the next letter
a sharp turn here

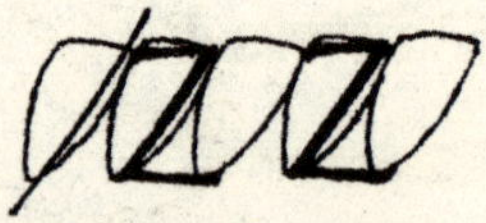

Joined letters are best for handwriting. In other cases unjoined letters are better.

Joined letters are usually less easy to read. The joins are there to benefit the hand, not the eye.

9

Joining up

Before starting these joining-up exercises it is worth thinking for a moment about why you join up at all. Tests have shown that even the fastest print cannot beat joined-up letters. A cursive hand tends to look more mature too.

Some people think that they can get away without joining up at all. Others join up too much.

This paragraph is addressed to those who think that cursive can never be as fast as their own quick, separate letters which look so economical. In fact they involve a lot of wasted movement that slows you down. It is not a good idea to have to lift and put down your pen every time you move it from the end of one letter to the beginning of the next. It is not just lifting and lowering, but the constant stopping and starting that causes jerkiness in the movement. This is what stops you from writing as fast as you are able.

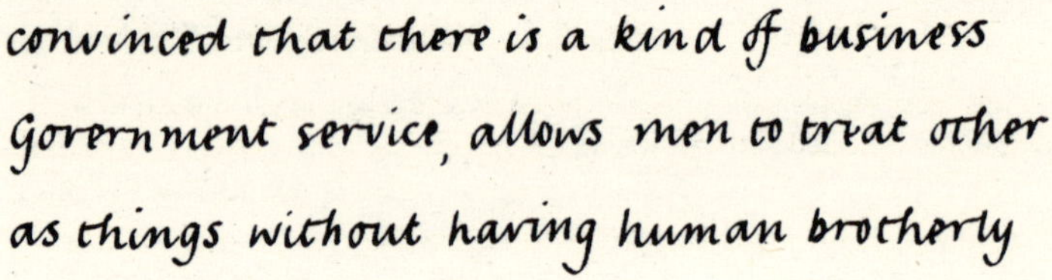

A good cursive hand can be both legible and fast.

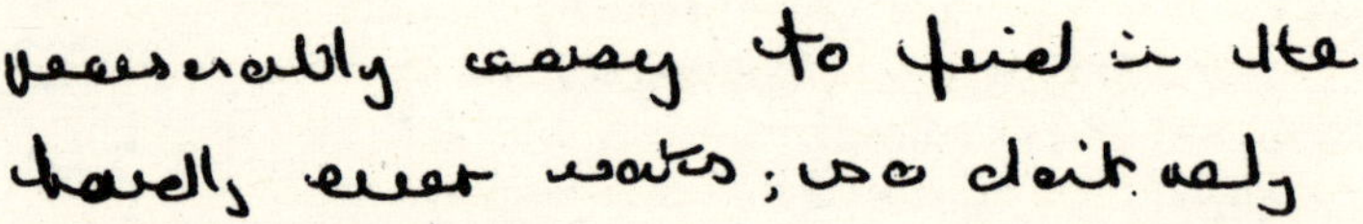

Joining strokes must be correctly formed. Otherwise words are illegible, however decorative a pattern the writing makes.

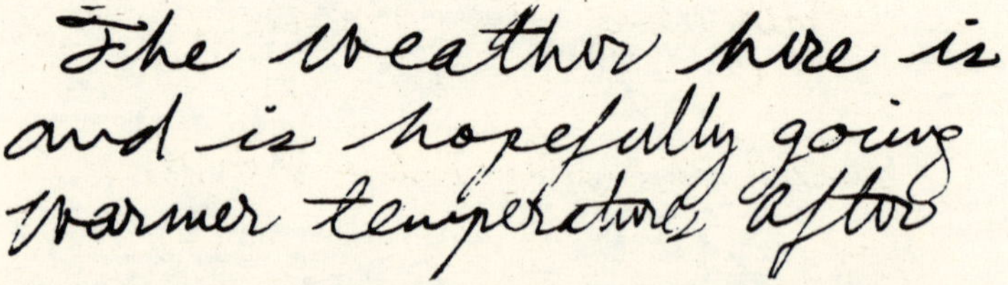

This writing would be much easier to read if the entry and exit strokes were simpler, and if the writer gave himself a break in the middle of long words.

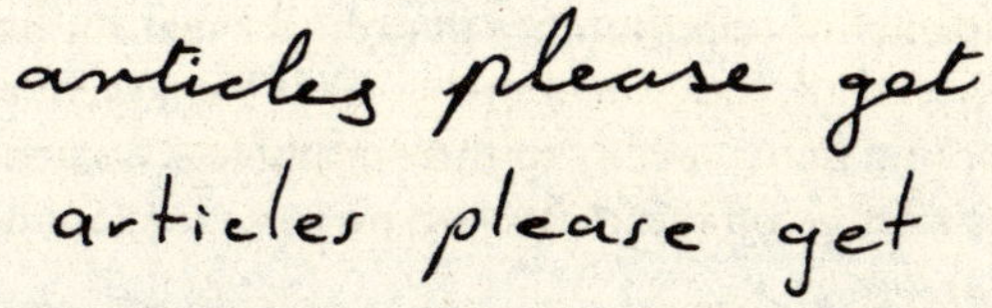

David's problem was that he had been taught to join up every letter every time. He had rebelled and gone back to printing.

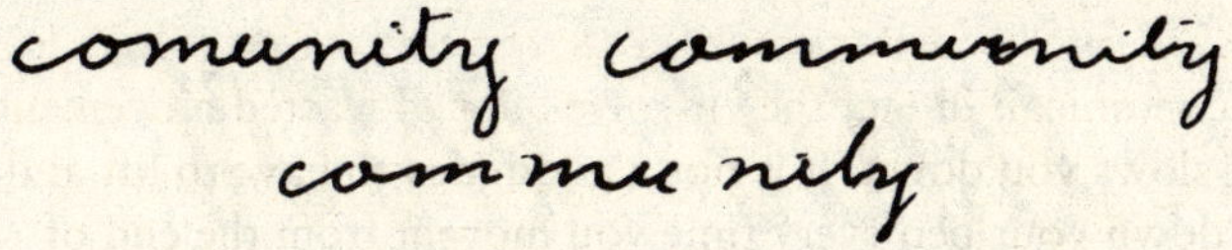

Not only did the continuous joining distort his letters and slow him down, but it muddled up his spelling too.

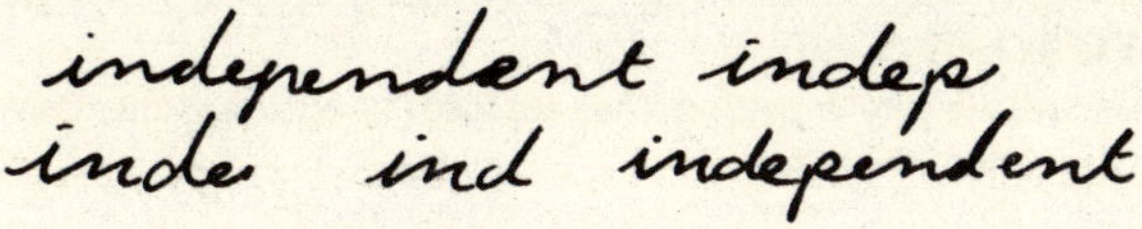

He was much happier when he was shown how to take a break in the middle of long words. It helped both his writing and his spelling.

This paragraph is addressed to those who join up everything they can. You may be overdoing it. Your hand needs to move along the line. It does not glide along as you write. It is a good idea to lift the pen every four of five letters. Look closely at your own writing and see what you have been doing. Even if it looks as if every letter is joined, there are probably breaks from time to time. If there are not, then there is usually an illegible jumble by the end of a ten- or twelve-letter word.

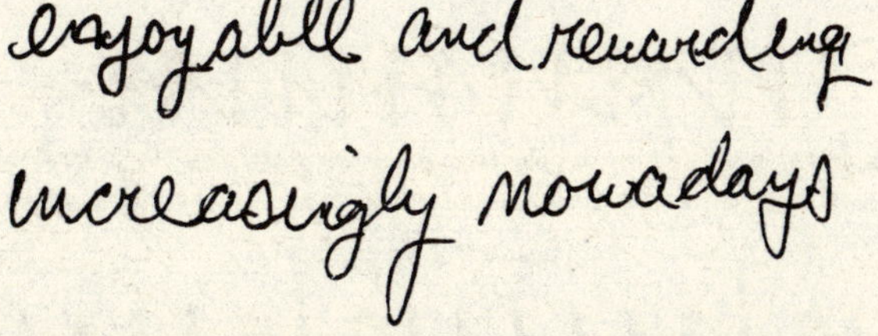

This hand worked much better when the writer took a penlift every three or four letters. Look what happened to the letters in 'increasingly' when he tried to write it in one go.

There are plenty of opportunities in ordinary text for natural penlifts. First of all, there are word breaks. Then there are letters that do not join up so readily to their neighbour. Sometimes your hand stops after a complicated letter, or when you are not quite sure how to join.

Join when it is comfortable for you, and your writing will have a better chance of being legible.

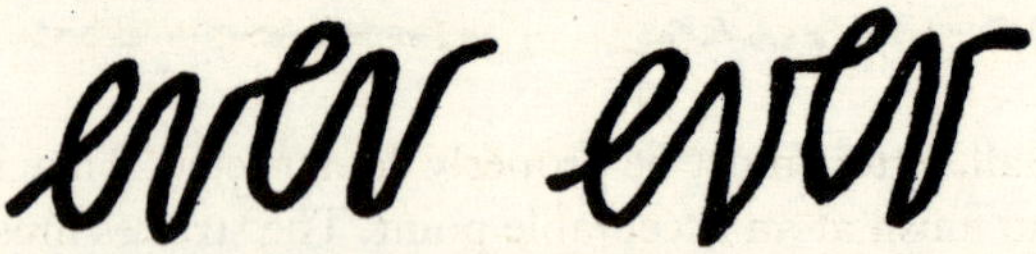

There are some letters that can look alike when they are joined up. **v** and **r** can get confused unless you are careful.

FLOW EXERCISES

These exercises are very important. They are made up of simple lines and arches and join easily from the base.

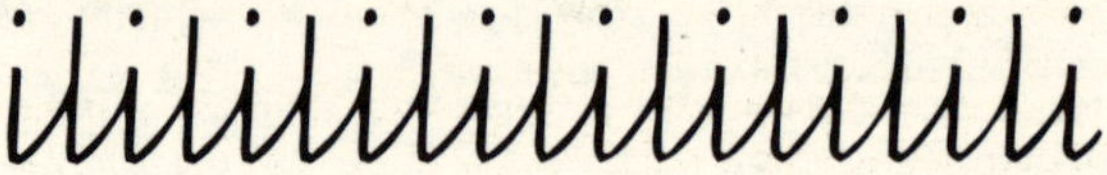

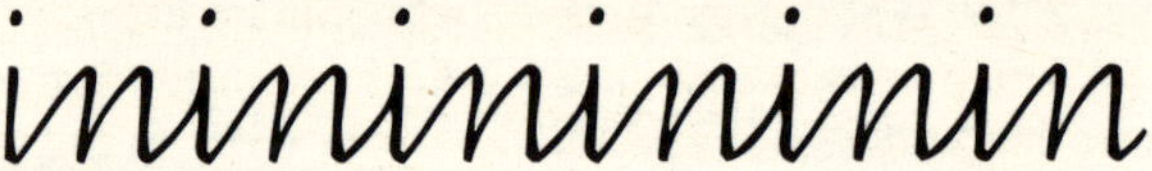

They can be used to loosen up, as an extension to the relaxing exercises on page 28.

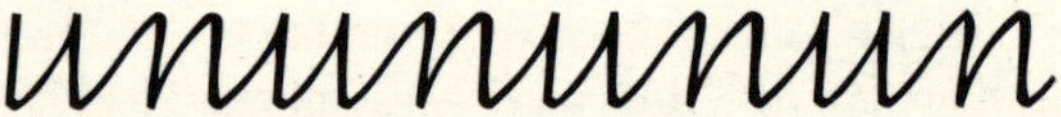

They are most useful in helping you to change from straight letters to a flowing cursive.

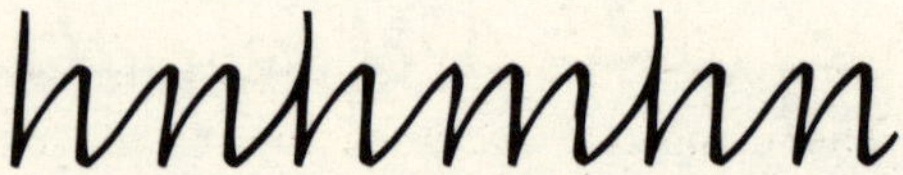

Their simple regularity helps develop regular joining strokes. Do several lines of each to start with, and repeat whenever you feel you are getting too static.

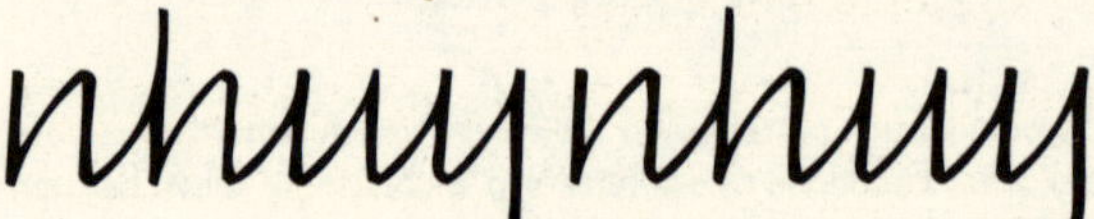

Learning to join up

How then should you learn to join up letters? There are right and wrong ways to go about this, and they need to be learned.

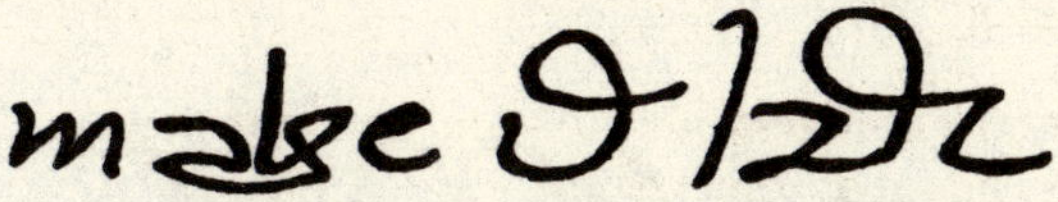

'make it late'. If you make your letters and joins too unconventional and take too many short cuts, no one will be able to read your writing.

First of all, letters must be properly constructed. They must start and finish at an acceptable point. The strokes must be written in the right direction. Otherwise they do not join up to make recognizable words. Some letters join from the top, and some from the base.

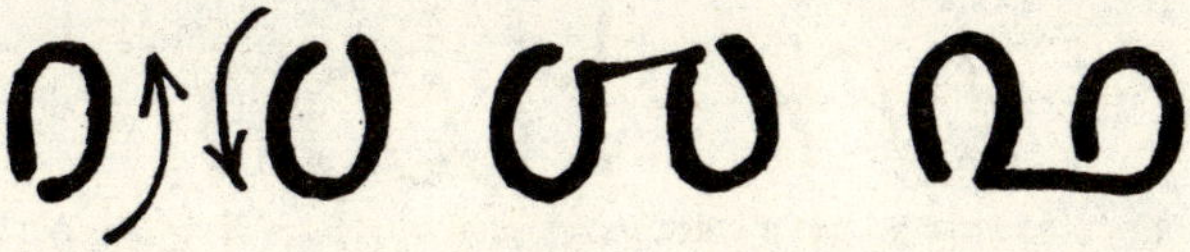

A separate **o** may be recognizable whether it starts at the top or at the bottom, and whichever way round it is written. But, when you join them up, you can see the difference. If you try and join two **o**'s from the bottom, the result is very odd.

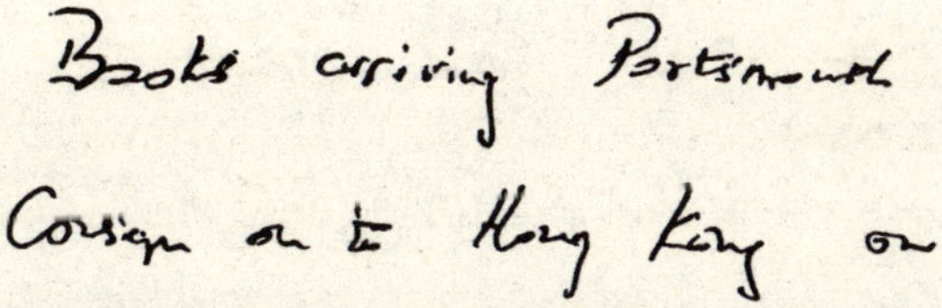

The **o**'s in this writing usually start at the wrong place and go round the wrong way. The first word and the last show this best.

If you write fast, separate letters, you may have learned to take short cuts. The most usual one is leaving out the first downward stroke of the letters **n**, **m** or **r**. Then there is no proper stem to join up to. If you try to join, you lose a stroke. So an **n** looks like an **i** and an **m** looks like an **n**.

This underlines the need for you to go back to pages 91, 92 and 96. They will show you how to construct your letters. Then you will be able to join up properly.

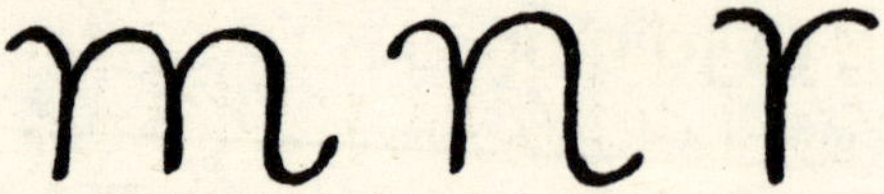

These letters must be formed properly, starting at the top and going down, then up and over.

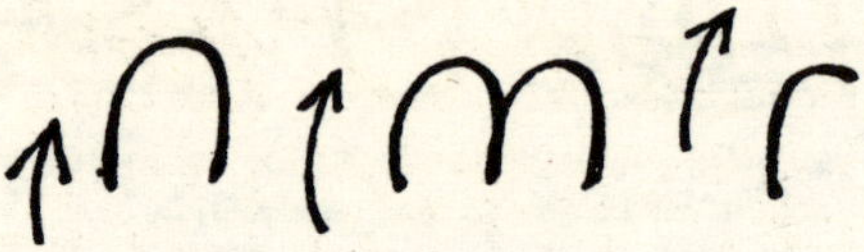

Some people start at the bottom and go upwards.

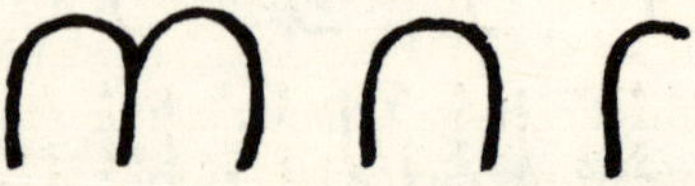

The separate letters may look all right, but they lack a vital stroke.

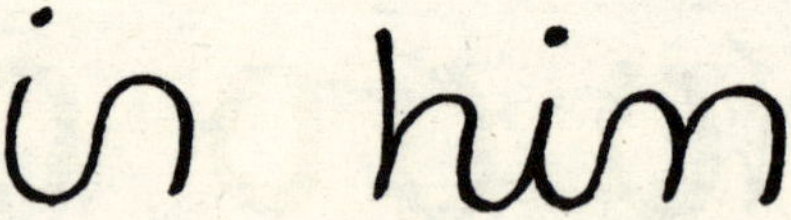

When they are joined up, the **n** is not recognizable and 'him' reads like 'hin'.

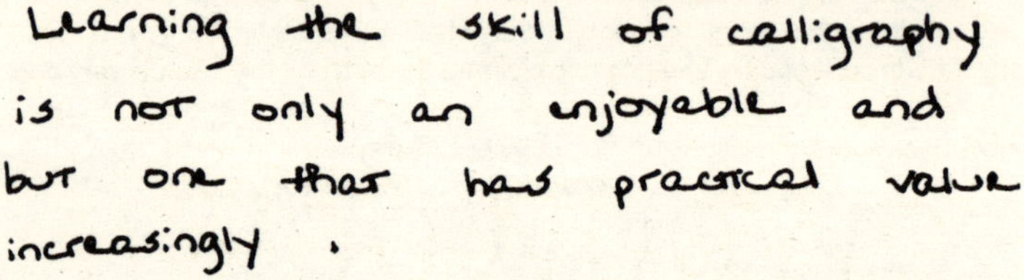

The **n**'s, **r**'s and **u**'s in this writing are all lacking a stroke. When an **a** joins an **n**, it goes along the base line.

Joining-up exercises

The exercises in this chapter consist of joined-up letters in pairs, threes and sometimes whole lines. They will get you into the rhythm of joining. They also make you practise the many different kinds of joins. You obviously need different strokes and ligatures to join differently shaped letters: to join straight letters to round letters, or short letters to tall letters. Then there are characters that join from the top and others that join from the base. These exercises use letters from the model in Chapter 8.

lhblhblhblhb

lhblhblhblhb

These exercises show simple joins to ascending or descending strokes.

iljiljiljiljiljiljilj

iljiljiljiljiljiljilj

These sequences would be useful in regulating a slant, too. You may need guidelines if you have trouble with the different heights of letters.

rorororororor

rorororororor

Now think about the letters that join from the top: **v**, **w**, **r** and **o**.

owoowoowo

owoowoowo

These exercises help you to practise the simple top-joining stroke.

wvwvwvwvw

wvwvwvwvw

Then you can go on to words like 'row', 'wood' or 'room'.

Descending and ascending strokes

A great many people write some or all of their ascending and descending strokes with a loop. The training alphabet in this book does not have loops: you will benefit from the clear lines and the discipline of the exercises. You can develop your own loops later on. The letters are designed so that, if the descending strokes are looped in a fast personal cursive, the ligature will be rhythmic and economical.

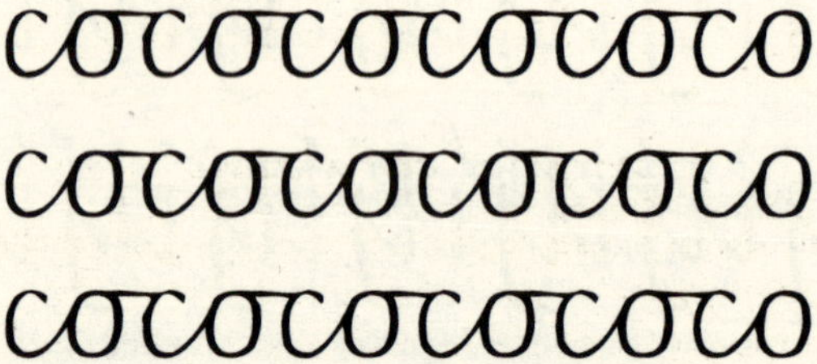

This exercise is getting a bit trickier. Here is a simple top join and then a reversing join. To join **c** to **o** you go over the top of the **o** and back again.

Joining to reversing letters

Some letters make the pen do strange things. It has to go one way and then turn back. This only happens when the letters are joined up.

The pen moves across the top of the letter **a** twice. The letters **a**, **d**, **c**, **g** and **q** are all reversing letters, and there are two usual ways of writing them. One way retraces the top stroke as the model does. Practise it for a while: it is very good to have the control that you need to do this exercise. The other way is more relaxed and uses a loop. Chapter 10 on personal modifications shows you how to deal with that.

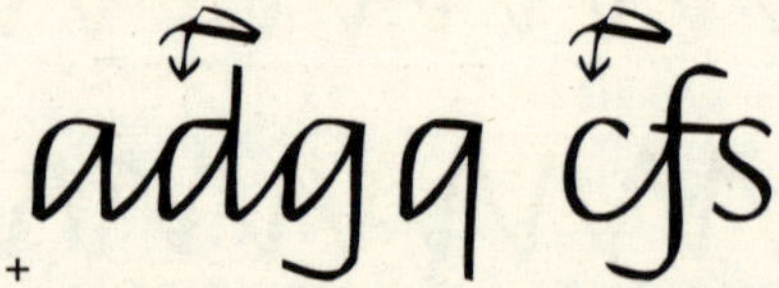

Joining to **a d g q**, **c f s** and of course **o** is done in the same way. At this stage of training you should go over the top of the letter and then retrace the stroke back and down again. This is very good discipline.

Some people avoid the problem by lifting the pen to move the hand along.

ca ca

Later on, when you get back to a personal hand, you may do this reverse join, or you can loop the join, or not join at all to round letters, just as you please.

Celia over dogwood

original catalogue

This writer sometimes chooses not to join to round letters, and at other times makes a very clean join to the top of his **a**'s. Note the two-stroke **e**.

When you are learning to join up, any writing is good practice. Nevertheless, it may be better for you to write the same line several times to reinforce what you have learned. Repeat the lines underneath each other. Concentrate on the joins. Compare the results to see how you have improved and carry on until you are satisfied.

The following exercises all concentrate on reversing joins.

dagadagada
adagadagad
dagadagada

cfcfcfcfcfcfcf
fcfcfcfcfcfcfc
cfcfcfcfcfcfcf

SSSSSSSSSSSSS
SSSSSSSSSSSSS

When you have mastered these and can do them neatly and are getting faster, then you are ready for the next stage.

elelelelelelele
elelelelelelelel

As there are two different **e**'s, there are two different joining exercises. Try them both and see which you prefer.

tititititititititi
ititititititititit

The letter **t** can join from its base or from the crossbar. Again, you should practise both ways. Remember **t** is not a very tall letter.

tititititititititi
tititititititititi

In your personal handwriting you will probably find that you join from the base sometimes and from the crossbar at other times. It can depend on what letter follows the **t**, and where it comes in the word.

Alternatives

In some joins there is definitely a right way and a wrong way of doing it. In others there are several ways of doing it. Take one of the simplest joins, that of an **i** to an **n**. Either it can go over the top and make a loop, or it can go straight to the top and make a point like this:

inininininin
inininininini

There are two ways of doing the simple join from **i** to **n** or **m**. In the first you go over the top of the downstroke, making a rounded join. In the second you go straight to the top of the downstroke and make a pointed join.

Most likely you are set in your own way of joining up, even though you never thought of this before. It really makes little difference which way you join those two letters, so you must choose.

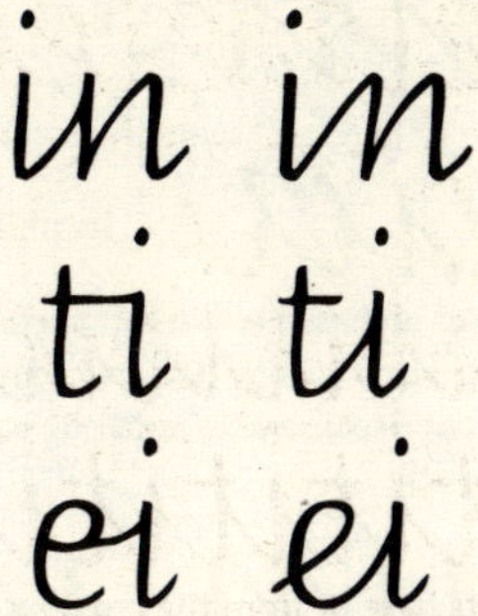

The alternative joins for '**in**', '**ti**' and '**ei**' are shown here.

Now the letter **t**. You probably know the old saying about not forgetting to cross your **t**'s and dot your **i**'s. This suggests that the writer joins the **t** from its base and then goes back to cross it and complete the letter. However, many writing masters suggest joining from the crossbar of a **t** like an **f**. Look again at your own writing. Maybe you do it one way, maybe another. Most people have a variety of ways that they join from the letter **t**. It depends on whether the letter is at the beginning, the middle or the end of a word, and even what letter comes next. Both ways of joining are shown here.

Next look at the **e**. The model shows two versions of the letter (pages 83 and 84). One is a single loop, the other is written in two strokes. If you have always used a one-stroke **e**, you are accustomed to joining it from the base to the next letter. The two-stroke e joins from the centre – and a very attractive and practical join it is. Try them both in different situations. You are likely to observe that the two-stroke **e** has certain advantages. You may like to take it up sometimes.

One thing that **will** make a difference to your writing is if you get careless with your arches. When you do these joining-up exercises, make sure that there is a difference between the **u** arch and the **n** arch. This is one of the most useful exercises towards building up a legible flowing cursive.

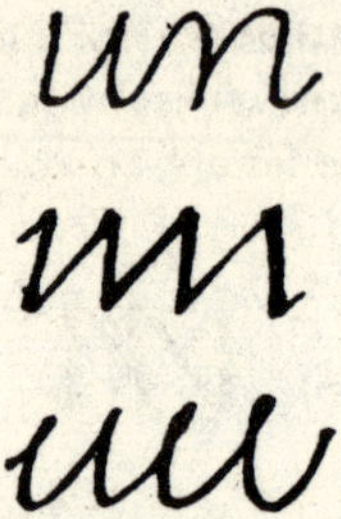

good

bad

terrible

If you are careless about your arches, **n** and **u** can become confused. The under and over are clear in the top sample. They have become a zig-zag in the second illustration, which may be just decipherable in a long word, but by the third they are a scallop, which is worse still.

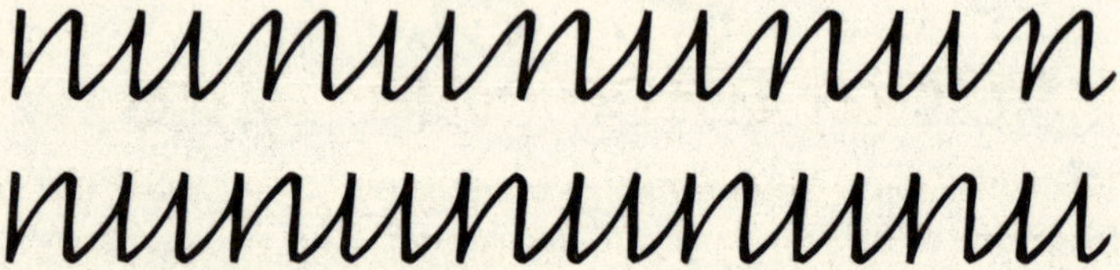

Now try several lines of 'nu' taking great care with your arches. Speed this up and try not to let your **n**'s become **u**'s.

Practising combinations of letters

For the next stage you should practise the most usual combinations of letters that you come across whenever you write. You can have fun making up your own sequences. Make yourself use the combinations that give you most trouble.

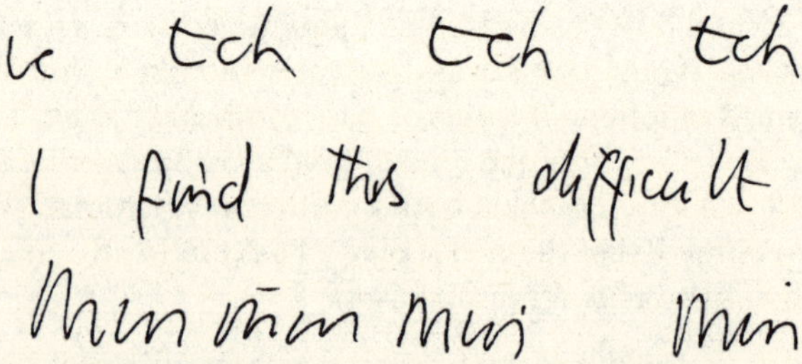

This writer persevered until her letter combinations joined smoothly.

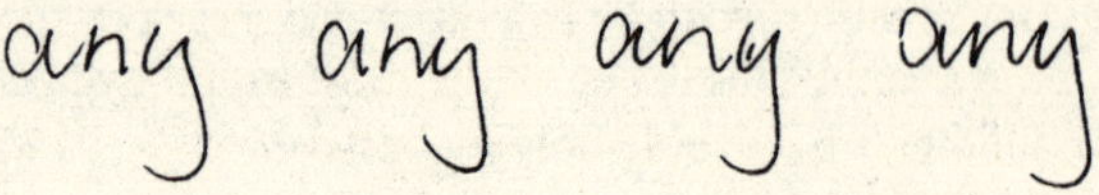

The next stage is to practise mixtures of all the different joining strokes. The best way of doing this is to write some of the most usual combinations of letters that are found.

ment sion est ious er

ant sh que and the

mic ous out our urs

ck al ance edge idge

lor ain able ple

ming ght ing

Here is a selection. Work on those that cause you the most trouble. Then think of some other combinations yourself and repeat them until they flow smoothly.

con-pro
ence que
est!
ext etc
in act of
any ned

ish tch
and if..
er-wha?
ough
ugh

It need not be too serious an exercise.

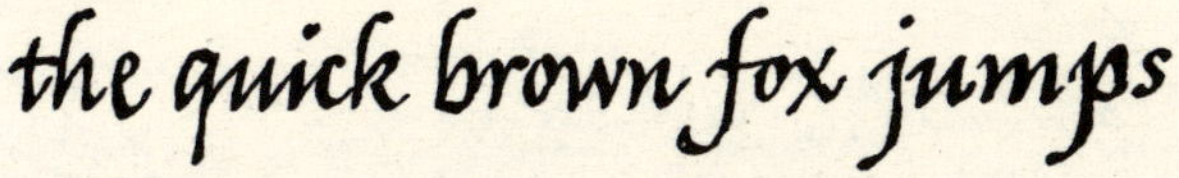

(2 minutes)

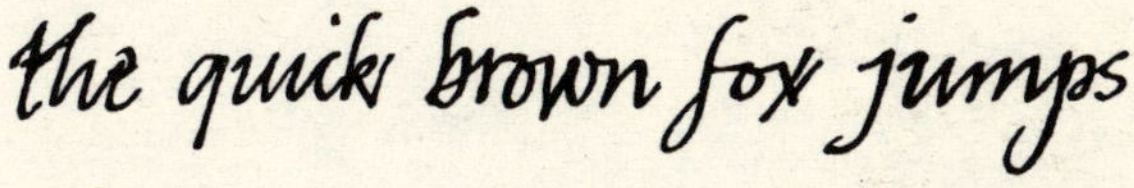

(1 minute, 10 seconds)

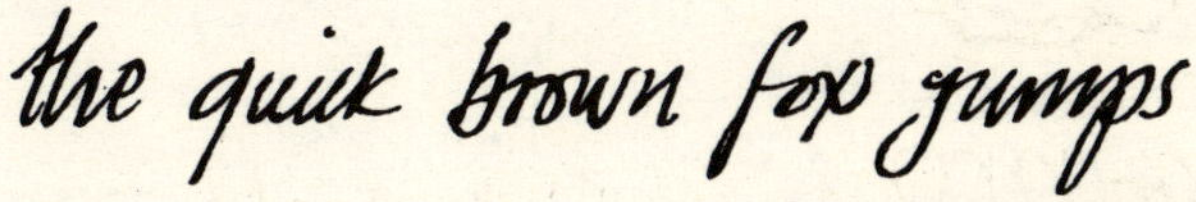

(44 seconds)

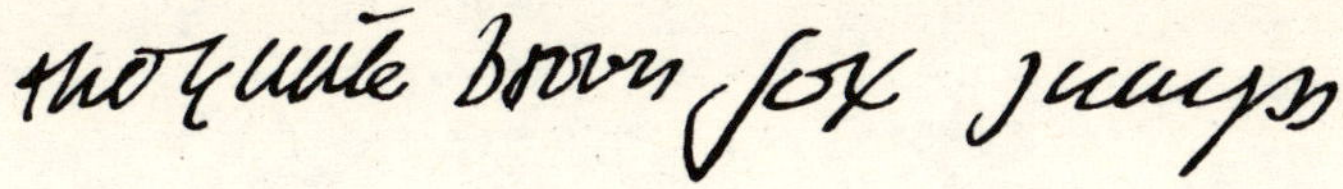

(18 seconds)

(4 seconds)

These examples show how careful writing changes and then falls apart at speed. The second attempt has more character than the first, and the third is perhaps the most interesting of them all.

10

Personal modifications

The training model in Chapter 8 is only a starting point. You will not be writing like that forever.

You should use it the way you would use a plaster cast if you break your arm: when the bone is healed and reasonably strong, you take the cast off. Your arm is the right shape, and it moves more freely.

You may be reading this book just because you want to change a few faults. Your writing may already be flowing and fairly mature. Quite likely you will have been influenced by the model so you will find your handwriting has changed. It may go on changing as you speed it up. After all, if you have gone through the book, you will have learned quite a bit about how handwriting works and will have taken up some of the ideas.

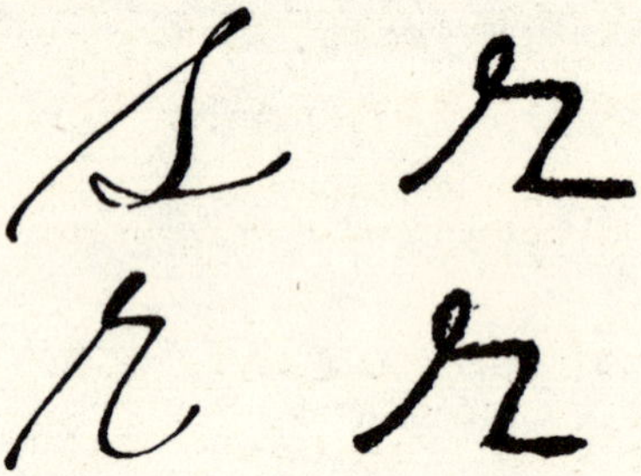

Make sure that your quick, personal letters are still legible. The first ***s*** and ***r*** are clearly different. But the same characters written at speed with a different pen are confusing.

If you stick too closely to any model, your writing will remain rather childish. It is the personal modifications that make a mature hand.

Maybe you have been searching for more help. Then you may have needed the model to retrain the construction of your letters. That will have been a straightforward but time-consuming exercise. Perhaps you have needed to practise all the basic joining strokes that lead to recognizable ligatures and cursive writing. If you have followed the model closely, the writing that you are now producing is a clear and basic kind of hand. It is clean rather than characterless, but may be almost childish. If so, this chapter is important to you. It shows how to develop a mature personal style.

Three things must be considered:

1 What angle is best for you?

2 How wide do you like the letters in your new handwriting to be?

3 How do your letters change when you join them?

This last is the most complicated part: how you add to or take bits away from the model so your writing flows more easily. This makes it your own personal hand.

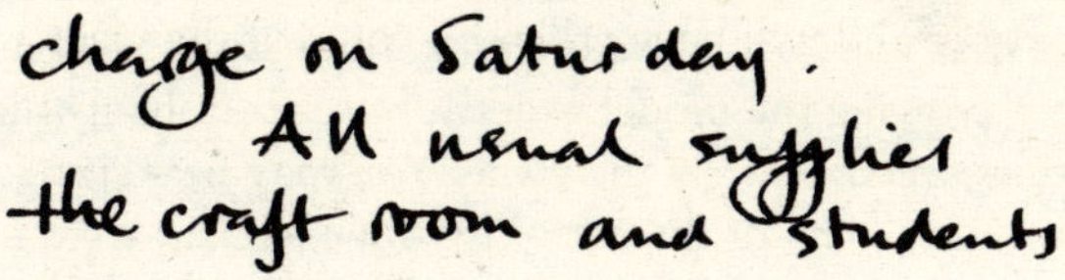

Victor lost no time in changing the proportions of his **s**. This is most noticeable in the capital letter on the top line. He enjoys extravagant **pp**'s.

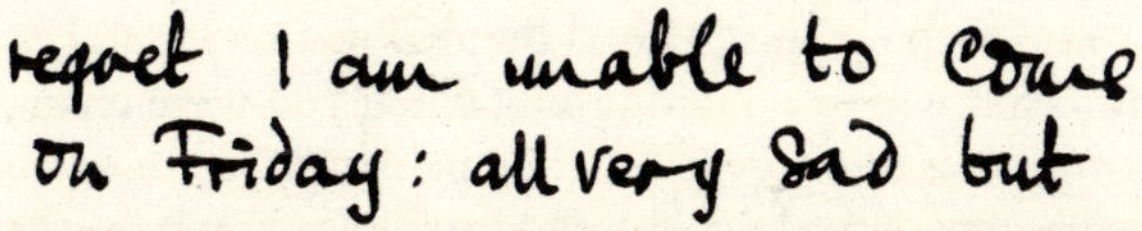

A horizontal emphasis is so natural to Grace that it would affect her writing whatever model she chose.

Here is an exercise for you. Write a sentence carefully in your normal hand. Do it again without lifting the pen anywhere. Do it a few times getting faster and faster until it gets totally illegible. There is a reason for this. Your handwriting has a different look when you write fast. It has a different shape for different functions. It can be just as legible when you hurry, and often more interesting.

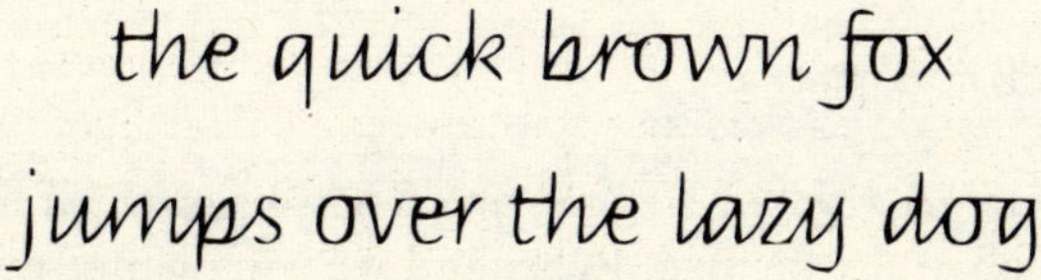

Stage 1 Careful writing.

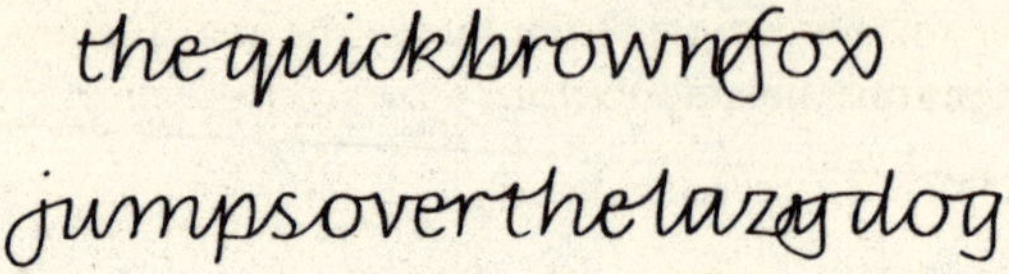

Stage 2 Careful writing without penlifts.

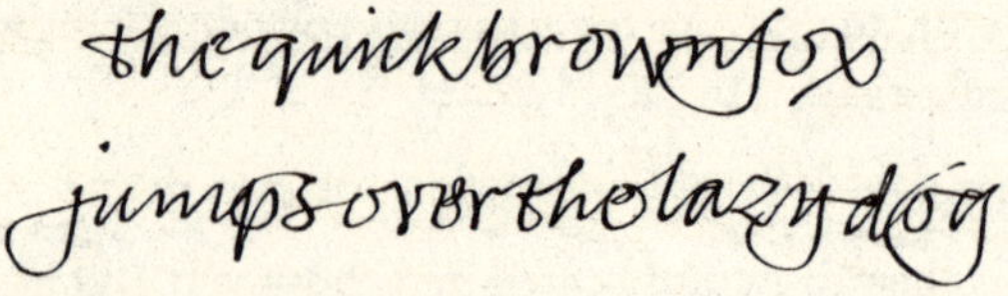

Stage 3 Writing at speed without penlifts.

You can find some clues to your own style if you examine the exercises that you have already done. You may think that you have been copying the model exactly, but it is unlikely that your letters are absolutely the same. You may be writing at a different slant: some of the early rhythm exercises were meant to show up your natural slant. Then, no matter how you try, your own letter shapes will show through from time to time: you may have rounded the tops of your **a**'s and **g**'s, or narrowed down some of the letters. This is the real you trying to get through. That was not a good thing when you were trying to copy the model. But now is the time to encourage this freedom. By this time you have had enough discipline. You have the correct movement. You know the basic joins. You are using a pen that suits you and that you enjoy writing with.

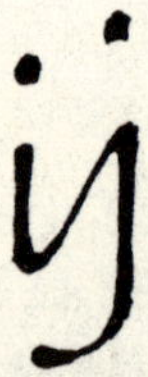

How you dot your letters reveals more about you than you think. When you are in a carefree mood the dot tends to wander. Do not put it too close to the downstroke. If you want to take special care, remember that, for balance, the letter **j** needs more distance.

Now try to get your writing moving freely, using the training that you have already had. Relax and see what happens.

Try this exercise: write an entire line without a single penlift. Do not even lift your pen to dot your i's. The overall effect is probably a bit odd.

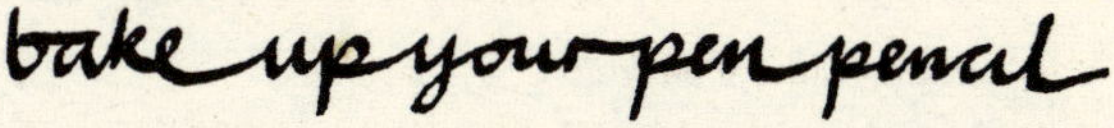

A student demonstrates the exercise that makes you write a line without lifting your pen from the page.

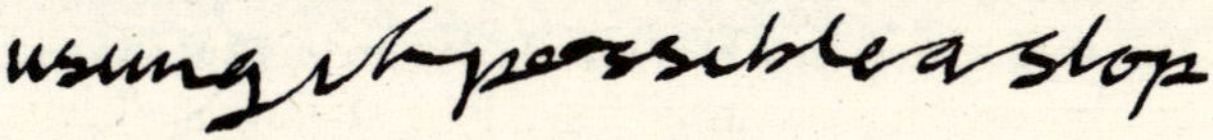

The faster she went, the more illegible it became.

The do-not-lift-your-pen exercise: how it worked

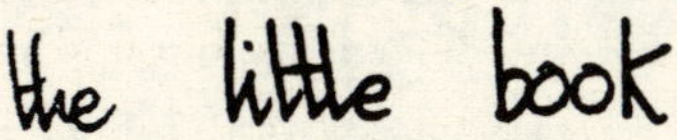

The top line shows a sample of handwriting that suffers from problems in joining. Even where it looks as if it joins, it does not really do so.

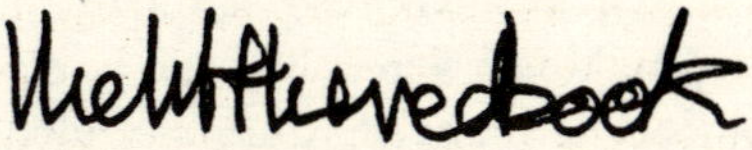

'The little red book', written without a penlift.

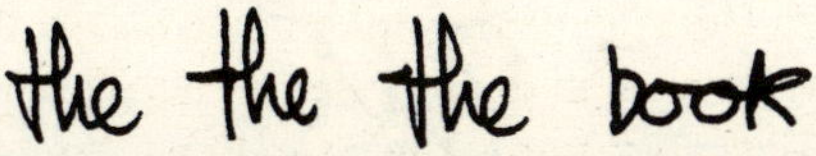

Examining the scribble, Nicholas found his personal solution to the 'th' join and could not stop practising. The 'oo' join needed a bit of refining.

This magnificent tangle reads 'fourfivesix'.

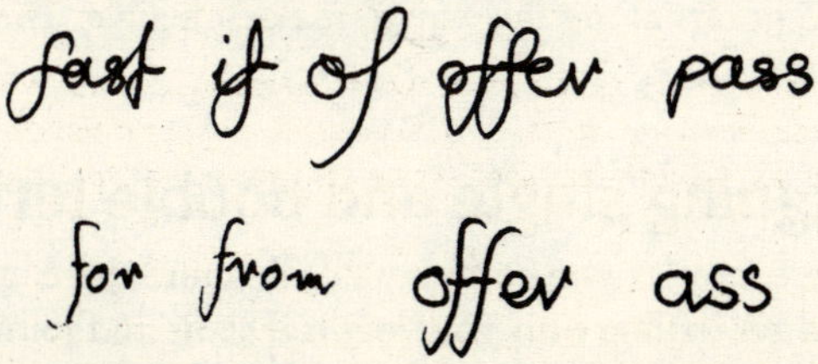

From this he developed some highly workable f's and s's. (The bottom line shows what he was doing before.)

Don't worry. Once again it is only an exercise, not what your writing should look like in the end. Next write the same line again. As before, do not lift the pen, but this time you should write much faster. It will probably look even stranger than it did the first time.

Now take a long hard look at it. There should be some f's and s's around. In the model they were simple shapes and were not joined. Look and see how you have simplified or added to them at speed. If this exercise has worked, you are getting closer to having your own handwriting. Then look at your **g**'s. In the model these did not join up to the next character.

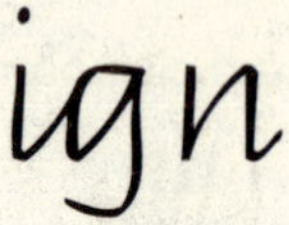

The **g** in the model does not join. When you want to write fast, you should join them or not, just as you please.

You must make a loop at the bottom if you are going to join, otherwise you are making a letter than can be mistaken for a **q**. The point is not just the shape of your descender but how you make the letters flow.

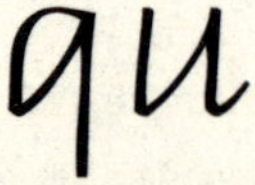

Please note that **q** joins in a different way from **g**. Similar letters need careful handling to avoid confusion.

There are many ways of looking at the alphabet. Here we are looking at movement. At this stage we could say that writing is a beautiful movement pattern, a zig-zag with a lot of good recognition points along the way to make it legible. That's all there is to it.

Redesigning single and double letters

After these exercises you still may not be quite there, although you should be settling into your natural slant and joining letters in a freer way. You have learned to write with an even rhythm. You are making the choice of where to join letters and when.

Now you may find that there are some characters which need redesigning to fit in with your new way of writing. The letters **f** and **s** are always interesting; so are word-endings like **ing**. The speed exercises may have given you some ideas of short cuts that suit you. Here are some more.

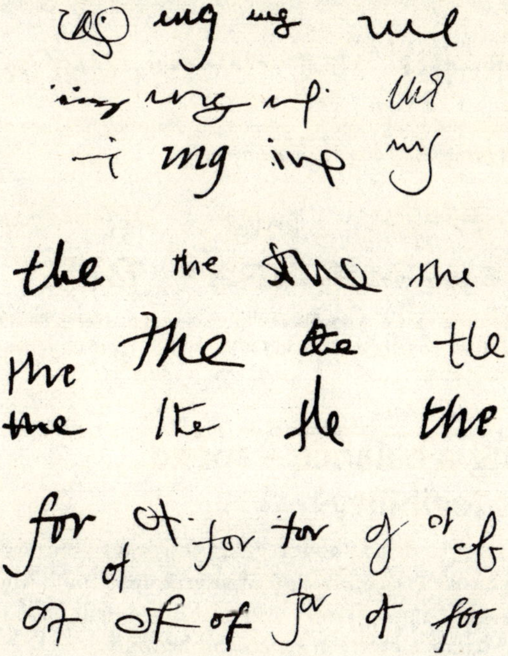

The amazing diversity of simple things!

The three groups are a selection of the different ways people write '-ing', 'the', 'of' and 'for'.

What makes them so personal is what is added and what is left out.

Double letters – two of the same, side by side – need not be a problem. They can be an opportunity for a personal touch. You do not have to write both of them exactly the same, and you can think of them as a single symbol. Once again it can depend on what letter comes before or after – for example, a double **s** is determined by the first stroke.

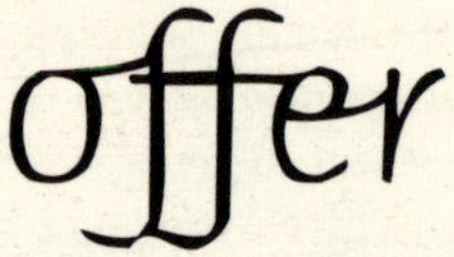

The model suggests simple joins. There is no need to do them by the book. The two personalized versions offer different solutions. One joins a double **f** according to the model. The other crosses both letters with the same stroke.

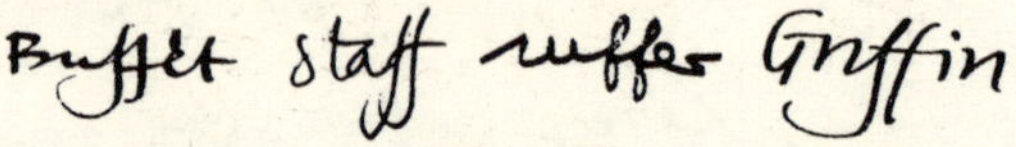

Double f's leave plenty of scope for individuality. Here you have one of the best excuses that handwriting offers to make a flourish.

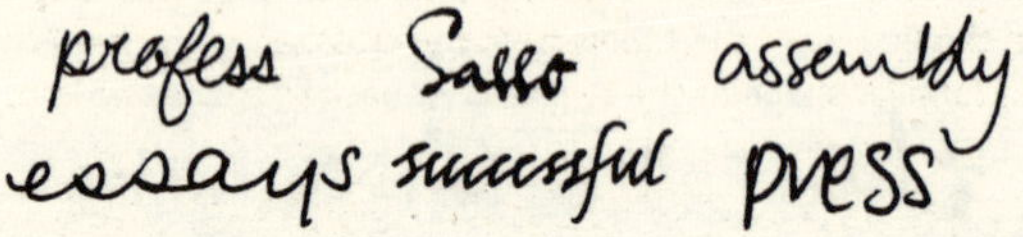

The complex movement of a double **s** so often causes problems. People find different solutions, sometimes breaking in the middle. There is nothing wrong with not joining at all.

Striking a balance – speed versus legibility

You will have to decide how regular you want your letterforms to be. If you write quickly, you obviously lose some legibility (even though it can still look very nice). You will have to find your own balance between speed and legibility.

If you want to write faster, this section is important. With enough speed, any handwriting falls apart. You are likely to find that, when you write in a hurry, the corners get widened out and the difficult bits are less carefully constructed. But now that you can make your hand do what you want it to, you can relax your discipline a little. If you have exercised enough, you will have noticed that your strokes and ovals get distorted in a different way from before.

This shows that your new habit of trained and disciplined writing relaxes into fluency. Your untrained hand just went to pieces.

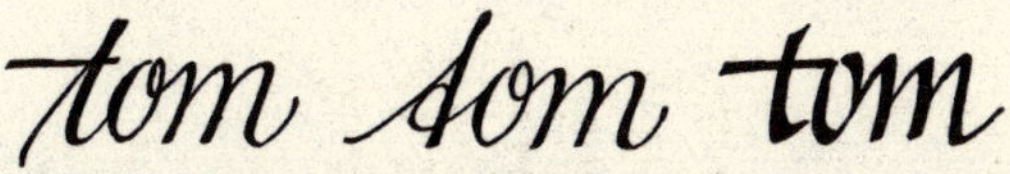

Here is an illustration of three forms of the letter **t**. The first joins out of the downstroke: the crossbar is added afterwards. In the second, the crossbar has been turned into a loop that joins to the next letter. In the third, the crossbar comes after the downstroke and makes the join.

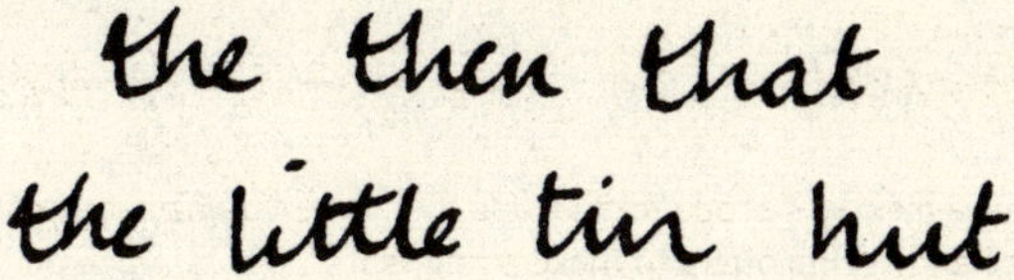

After the exercise on the top line a student tried a sentence with single and double **t**'s. In the first word the **t** joins from the crossbar as she has just learned. With the less familiar shape of the **tt**, she went back to a baseline join.

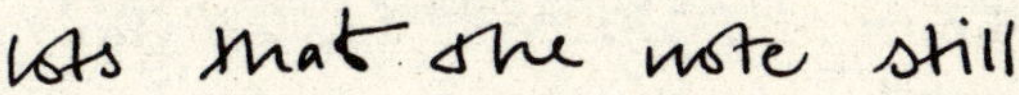

Judy's **t**'s are very interesting. She has an upwards diagonal crossbar join, and a horizontal one. Then she has two movements to get the pen from the downstroke to the crossbar. At the end of the second word she needs two loops. In the first letter of the third word she does with one.

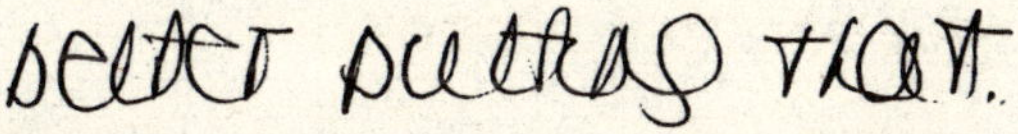

In this remarkable writing the normally spiky letter **t** gets rounded when it is doubled.

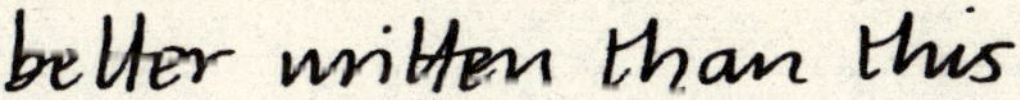

This writer has decided that joining from the crossbar works better. In his double letters he economically makes both downstrokes first and joins them both from the crossbar.

A silly **g**

11

Capital letters

Up to this point you have been concentrating on the movement of writing. There are two kind of letters: the small ones and the capitals.

The small letters join up so the writing can flow. Therefore they can be written quickly without falling apart.

ABCDEFG
HIJKLMN
OPQRSTUV
WXYZ

Capital letters are taller than the small ones but not as high as the ascenders. An average text uses one capital for every 50 small letters. Therefore capitals do not need to have as smooth a movement.

Capital letters are not built for speed. The capitals were the first letters in the Latin alphabet. Everything else came later. Even though they look very different, the small letters developed out of the capitals. This happened because people needed to write faster.

Capital letters are based on geometrical shapes. The **A** and **V** are obviously triangular. **O**, **Q**, **C** and **G** are based on a circle.

You cannot write squares and circles as fast as you can ovals and zig-zags – just try. That is how and why our writing has developed into its present form.

It is rather like driving a car. When you are in a city, you have to make sharp turns to go around a corner. To do this without going off the road, you must slow down. The same is true of capital letters. There is no need to hurry them, rather the opposite. They can be used to add impact and importance to your writing. They are not meant to join up either.

ABCD
EFGHI
JKLMN
OPQRST
UVWXYZ

Capitals are close to basic geometric forms (circles, triangles, etc.). If you look closely, you can see the rectangle in the letters **E**, **F**, **H** and so on. The centre crossbar of an **E** should be slightly higher than the middle of the letter. Otherwise it looks top-heavy. The lower crossbar of the letter **F** should be slightly lower than the same stroke on the **E**. The top bowl of the **B** should be a bit smaller than the lower one. The letter **R** has a slightly larger bowl than the top part of the **B**. And the **P** has a slightly larger bowl than the **R**. Proportion between height and width is important. Keep the **B** and the **E** narrow. The letter **N** fits a square and so does the **H**.

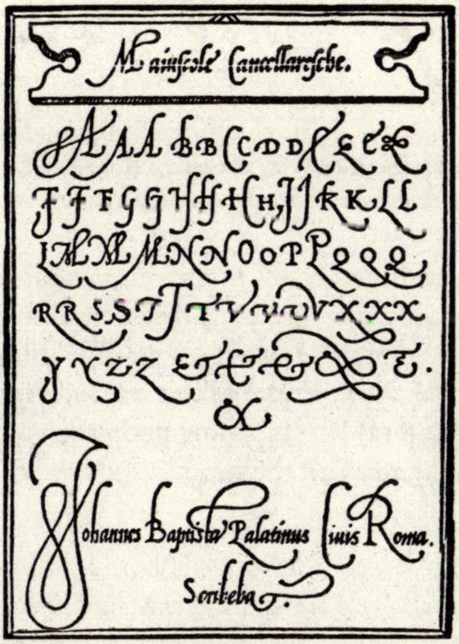

A panel of swash capitals from a book by the Italian writing master Giovanbattista Palatino, printed around 1540. Some of the characters seem a bit strange when we look at them today. They are fine for inspiration, but use them with restraint.

Here are some more swash capitals. Swashes are delightful but should only be used now and then. Practically any stroke can be extended. On the whole it is easier to control entry strokes than exits. Never put a dot over a capital letter I.

Nowadays we are urged to fill in any important form in block capitals. Presumably they are considered more legible than the average person's cursive. However, a strange thing is happening. People who spend a lot of time filling out forms are beginning to join up their capital letters. Some people are beginning to use joined-up capital letters all the time.

CAPITALS. IT GAVE ME MORE TIME TO 'THINK' WHILE I WROTE: QUALITY RATHER THAN QUANTITY, I USED TO THINK. BUT SINCE EVERYONE ELSE CHOSE TO WRITE IN UPPER AND LOWER CASE, I SUPPOSE I'D BE OUTVOTED ON MY LOGIC.

It is not a good idea to write everything in capitals, even if this example is rather nice. They are not built for speed.

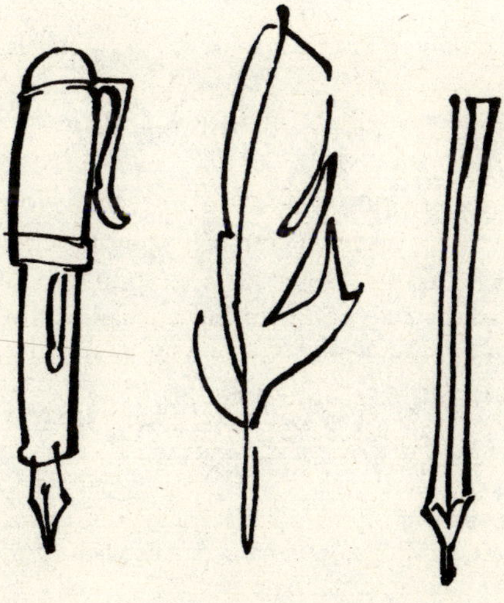

Part three

Before and after

Gail felt that her writing looked childish

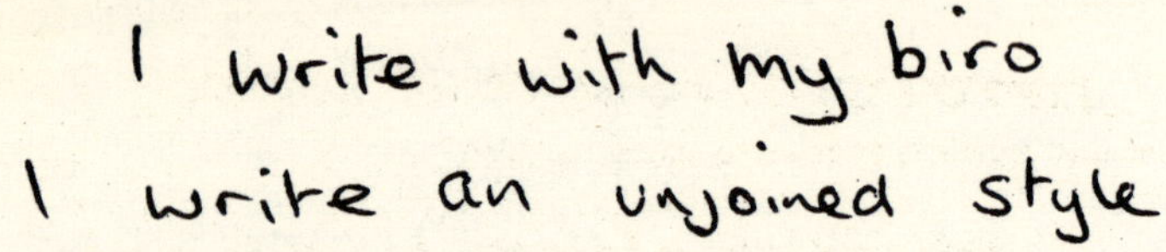

Her letters did not join up enough. They were correctly constructed at the stage shown here, but they did not flow.

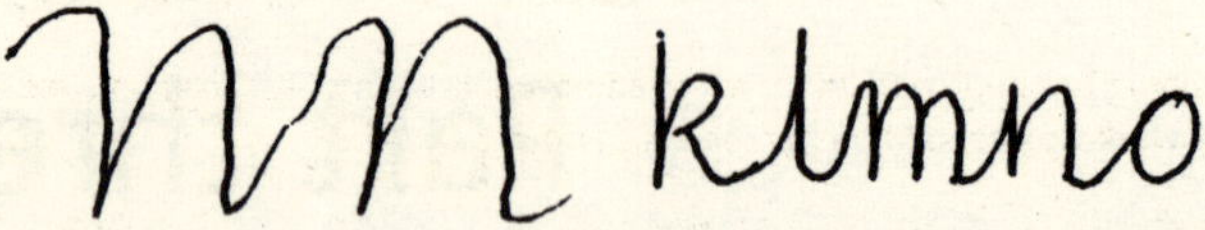

She tried on her own to retrain her writing. As a model she used a book that was meant for the teaching of young children. The model alphabet was too large, and she found that joining letters in alphabetical order was the worst way to learn.

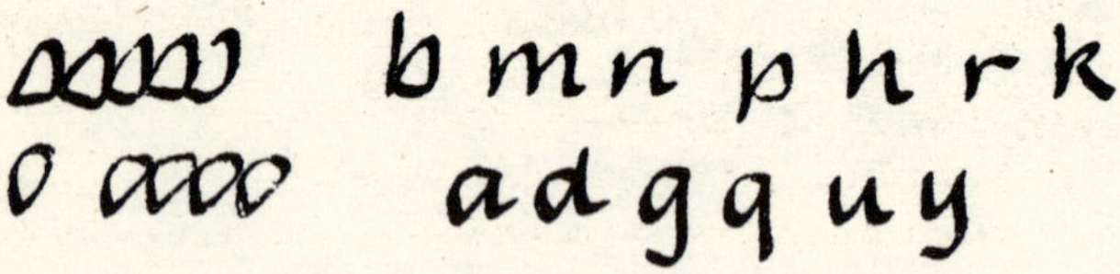

She discovered that letters were easier to master when they were in groups of similar strokes. She used the model alphabets in Chapter 8 and found that the smallest suited her best.

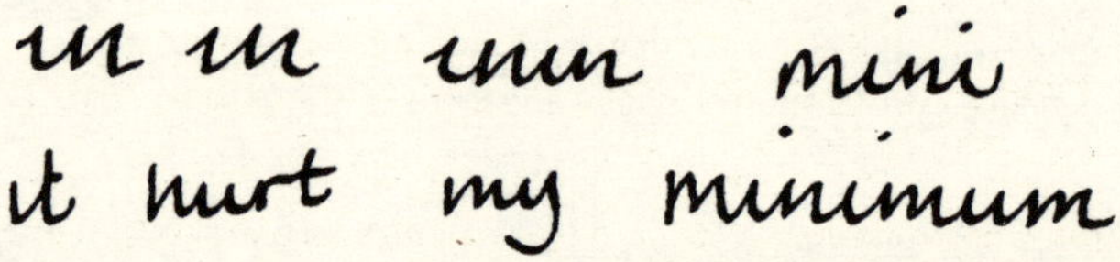

She learned joining in easy stages; the simple ones pointed the way. She tried various pens and chose a broad-edge nib.

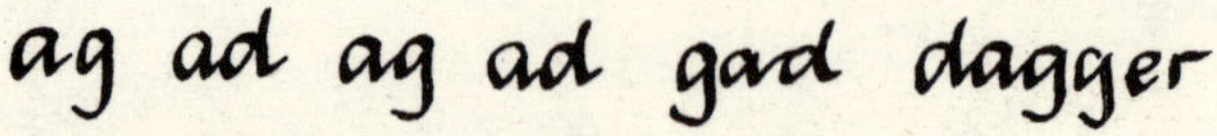

Once her writing began to flow she tackled more complicated joins, still in stroke-related sequences.

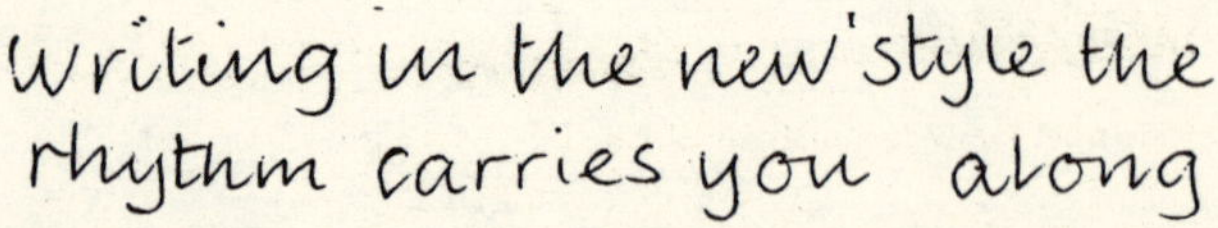

Gail kept very strictly to the model for a while. It was a very constructive mould for her own writing.

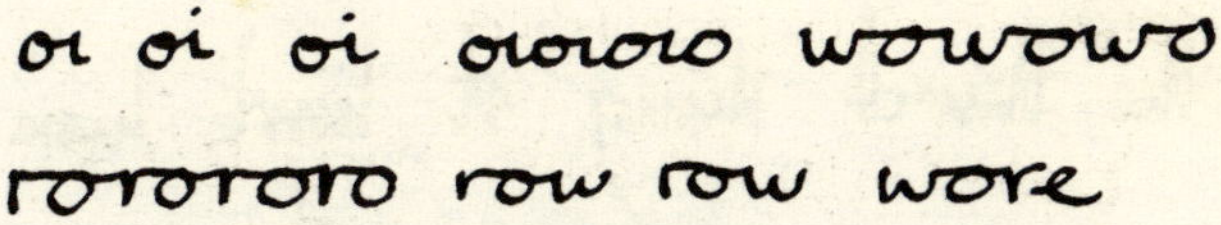

She used repetitive exercises to master top joins.

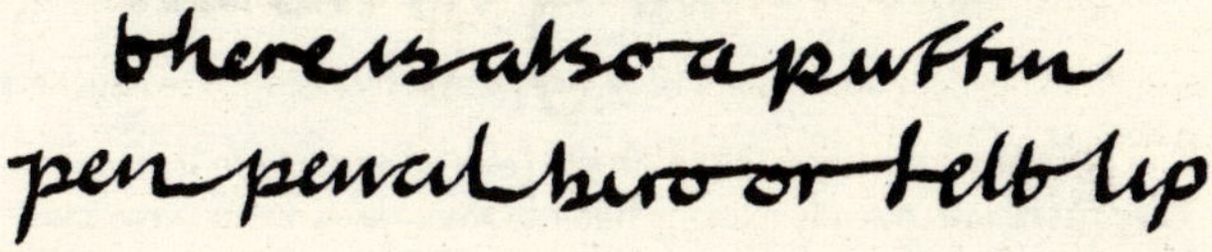

In refining her improved hand, she used no-penlift exercises. They showed that more work was needed on her letters **f** and **s**.

She chose a short **f** and looked into various ways of joining the letter **s**.

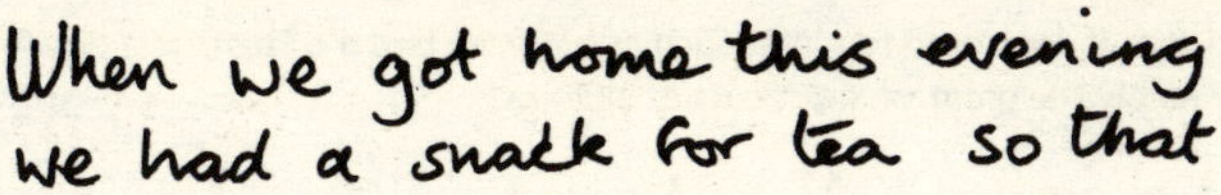

After a few weeks of keeping a diary, to ensure that she would practise every day, Gail had developed a really personal hand. It joins without effort, whichever pen she uses.

The result of two hours' analysis and treatment

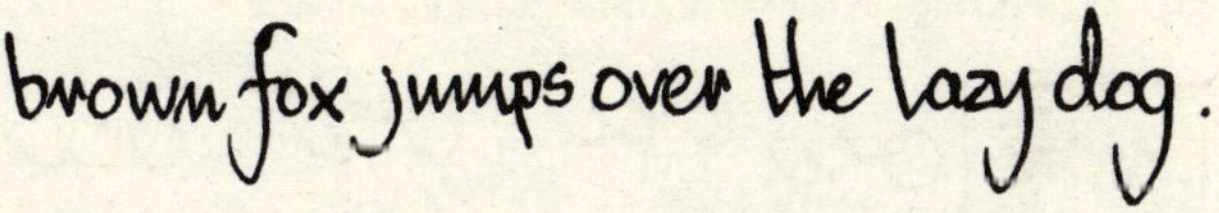

Nicholas wrote so slowly that he ran out of time in his examinations. Something had to be done. His writing looked decorative but was too slow because of wasted motion. It hardly joined up at all. Parts of his case are shown on page 127.

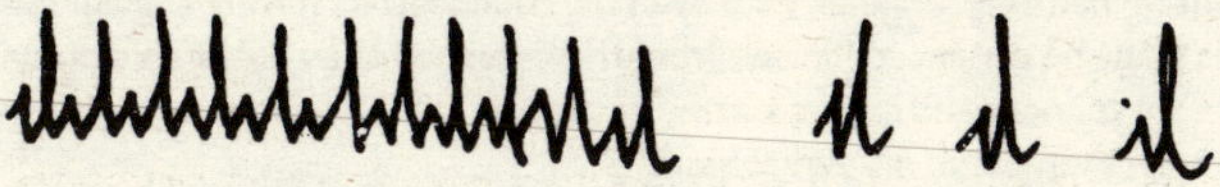

At the outset of his retraining his handwriting was extremely angular.

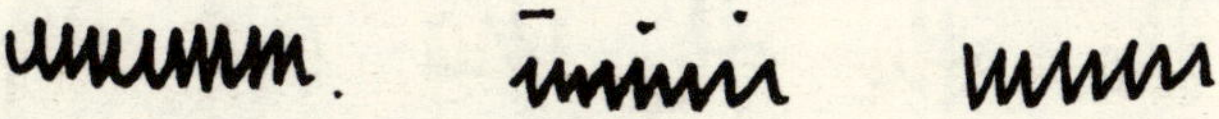

His letters **n** and **u** were indistinguishable.

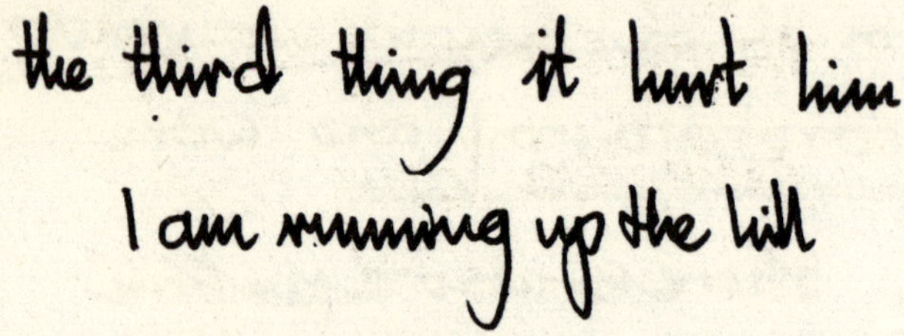

He had no difficulty in mastering the simple joins upwards from a preceding letter. They fitted into already existing habits. Other movements were more of a stumbling block.

He seldom, if ever, used top joins such as between two **o**'s. This was a pity. They are probably the greatest short cuts of all joins.

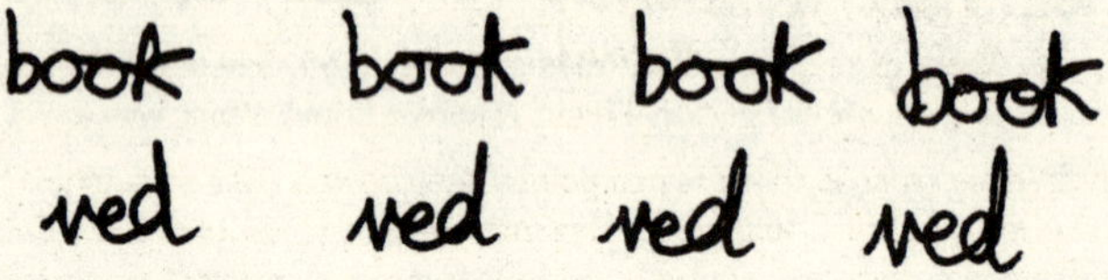

Nicholas had great success with his exercises. The more he practised, the freer they got. The next stage in his development was fundamental.

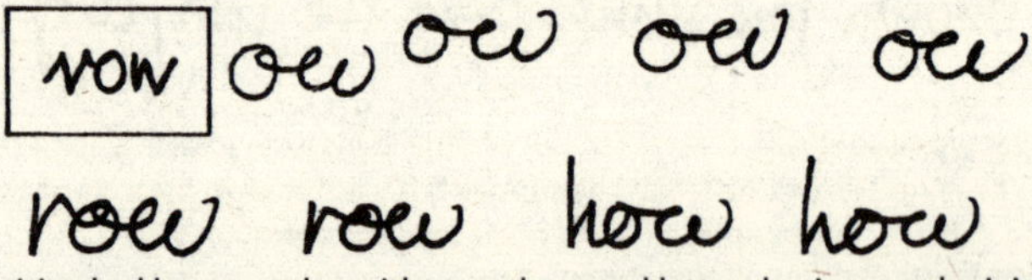

His writing had been angular, with even the round letters having angular joins. At this stage he distanced himself from the influence of an unsuitable model. His letters got rounder and curves started appearing in his joining strokes. Marked in a box is an example of his earlier work.

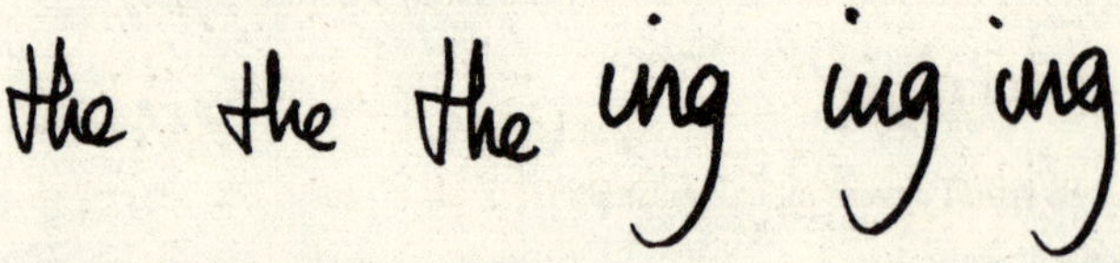

An exercise of continuous writing made him develop an increasingly rounded, flowing 'the'. His **n** arches benefited at the same time.

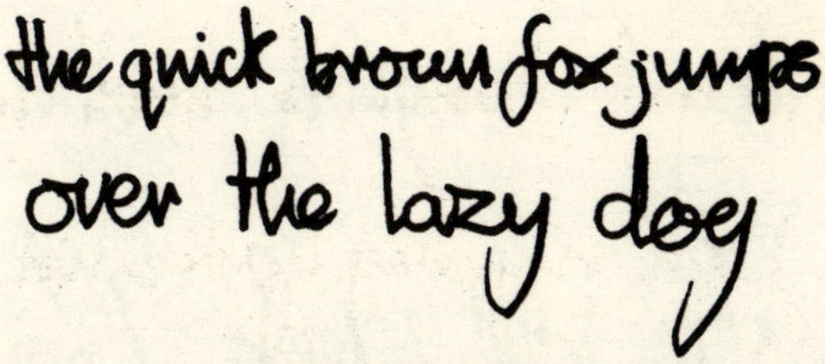

The final result is still Nicholas' writing. On the surface it looks pretty much the same. However, the underlying movement pattern has been transformed. This new handwriting can be written much more quickly.

Writing was painful for Julia

She is right-handed but wrote with a hand position that is usually confined to left-handers.

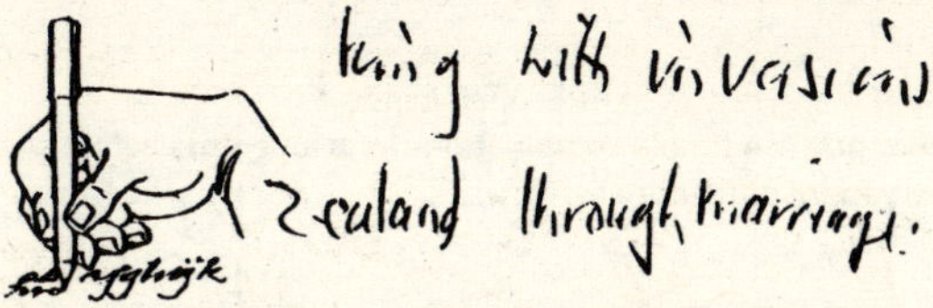

She twisted her wrist so that the pen pointed towards her. This turned her downstrokes into thrusts and her writing into a jagged staccato pattern. But her problem was physical pain. Her wrist hurt so much that she almost gave up writing altogether.

Her first finger and thumb sometimes crossed each other. She found a corrective plastic grip very comfortable.

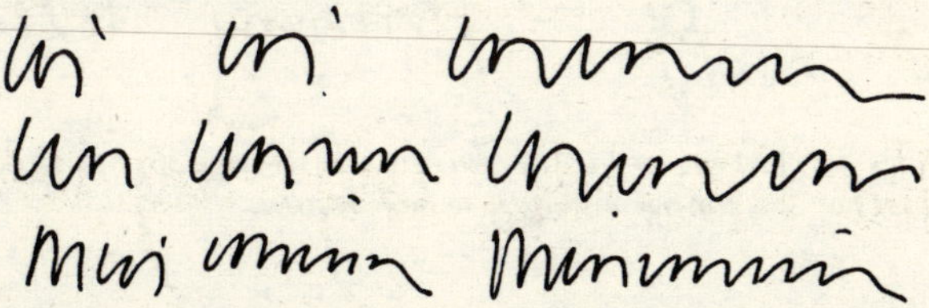

Changing a grip is very difficult. She could not expect to write whole sentences right away. A lot of relaxing scribbles had to come first. Little by little, her scribble exercises were turned into letters.

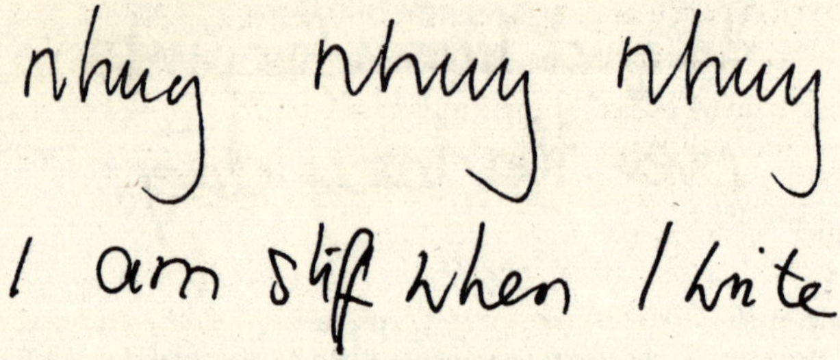

Julia is intense by nature and often needed reminding to relax.

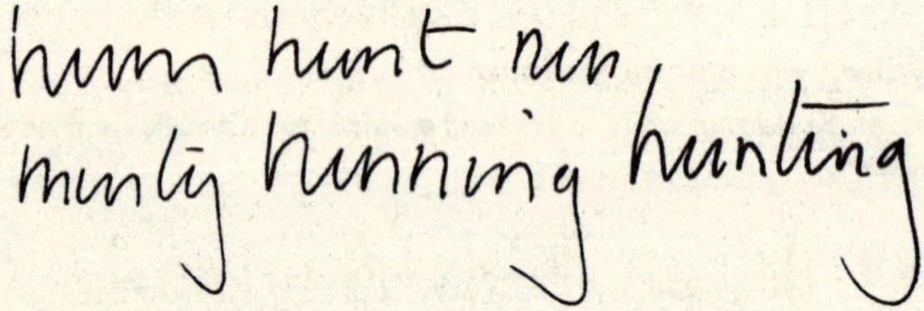

She needed to practise simple combinations for a long time before she could be allowed to try more difficult ones.

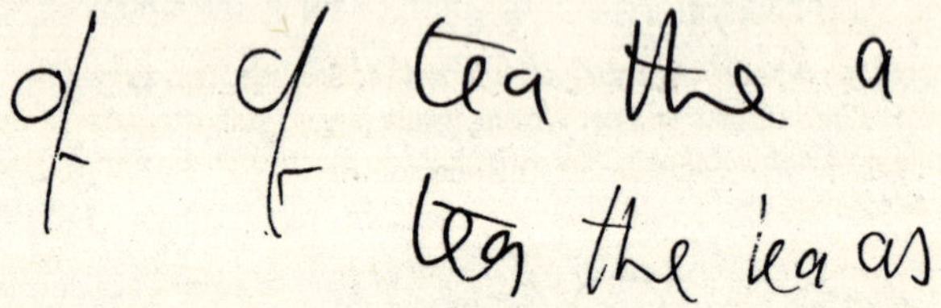

She liked exercises of frequent letter combinations as an approach to flowing letters. (Look how she dealt with her letter **a**: to begin with, it had no joining stroke, but after a few tries it joined happily to the **s**.)

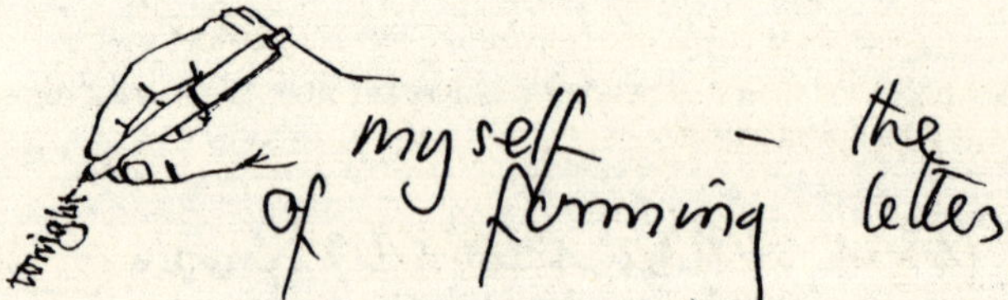

By the time Julia had got used to her new penhold (see page 36) writing no longer hurt her. She, and her writing, were more relaxed.

HOW YOUR PAPER AND PEN MAKE A DIFFERENCE

You must try a few pens to see what kind is best for you. The same is true of paper. Some kinds make your writing better than others. It could be useful for you to try this experiment yourself. You might be pleasantly surprised by the improvement in your writing.

▶ Pat likes to write with a ballpoint on firm paper

Scratchy cannot complete downstrokes

She tried a stiff cartridge and did not like it. Too scratchy.

not free flowing

She found a fibre tip; it did not work very well for her.

Indents paper

She tried newsprint. It was too soft. The pen dug into it.

usual biro not sympathetic paper

Hard bond paper took the ink well but was 'not pleasant to write on'.

This pen fine on this paper

She admitted that a fountain pen could write rather well but could not find anything better than her old ballpoint. Others find experimenting more rewarding.

▶ Gillian likes a fountain pen

Although she writes in italics, she prefers an ordinary nib.

(Uncontrolled) but quick.

She does not like ballpoints because they are difficult to control.

(blots, but feels quite pleasant. Picks up fibres).

Cheap, coarse paper blotted and feathered when she used her favourite pen.

refill edding (encourages untidiness) but easy to use.

She found a fibre tip easy to use but felt that her writing might deteriorate.

▶ Gail noticed how different pens and paper changed her writing

the pen flows over the paper it helps the rhythm

She likes a broad-edge pen on bond paper with a bit of 'tooth'.

paper makes a lot of differenc.

a pen with a cap on the bottom unbalances my hand

She does not like shiny paper. She does not mind a fibre tip but a balanced pen is important to her.

▶ **What keeps handwriting in shape when it is written at speed?**

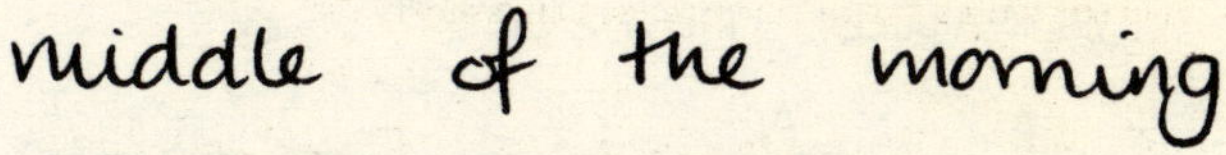

How do different hands behave when they are speeded up?

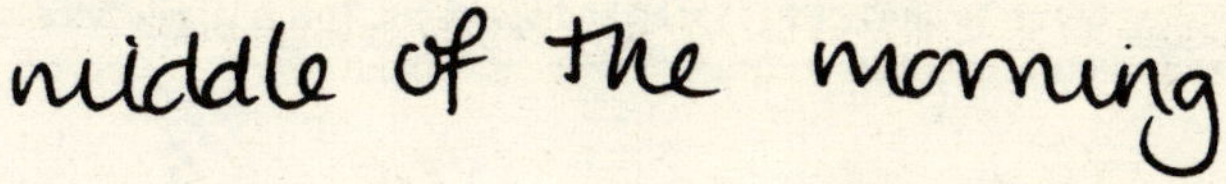

Louise has a smooth, economical movement in her writing. The **o-f** and the **t-h** joins work particularly well.

She was asked to write the same sentence many times and increase her speed each time.

As was to be expected, her writing got larger but, even when it went very fast, her writing remained vigorous.

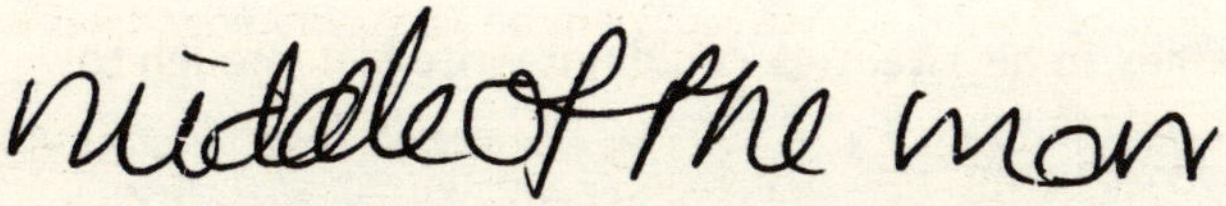

At full speed she wrote the sentence 21 times in the fixed time span.

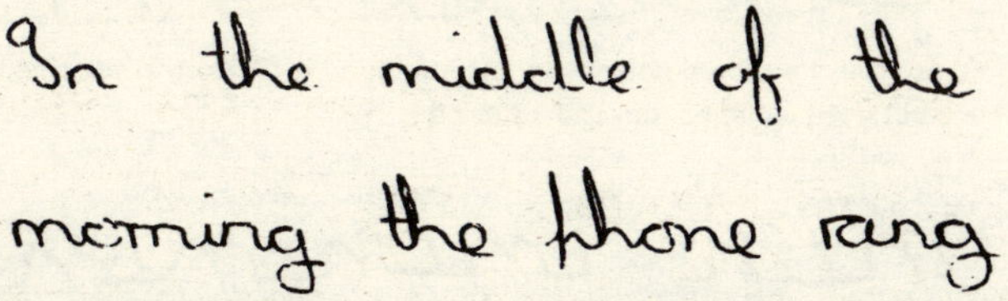

Rachel has a round, looped hand with some decorative squiggles. When it is written slowly, it serves its purpose. It is legible. The writing movement and co-ordination are suspect, however.

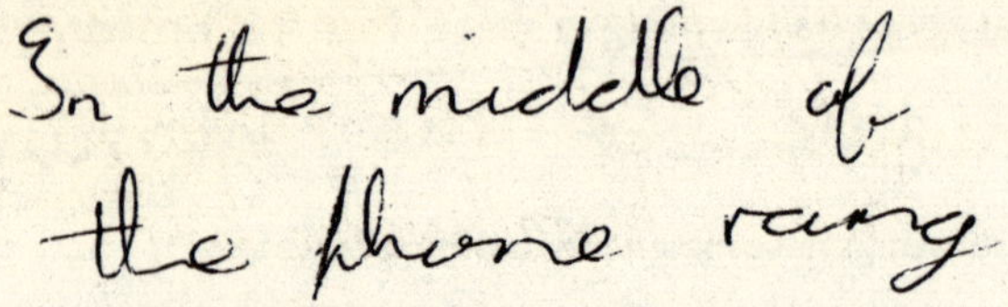

The writing becomes unhinged at speed and opens out. This is largely because the hand still tries to follow its usual movement without taking any short cuts.

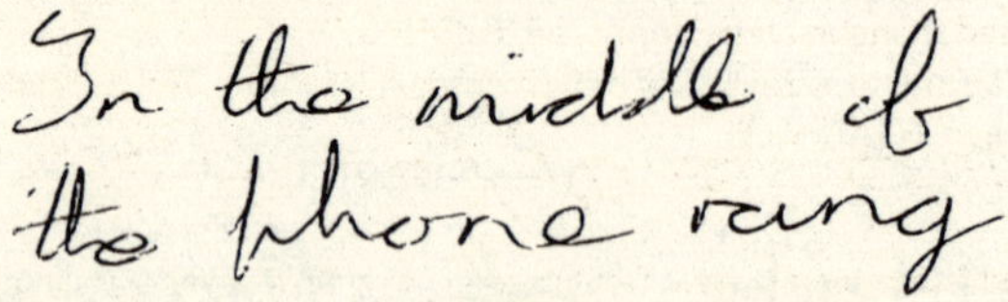

During the fixed time span of the experiment, she only managed to write the sentence 15 times.

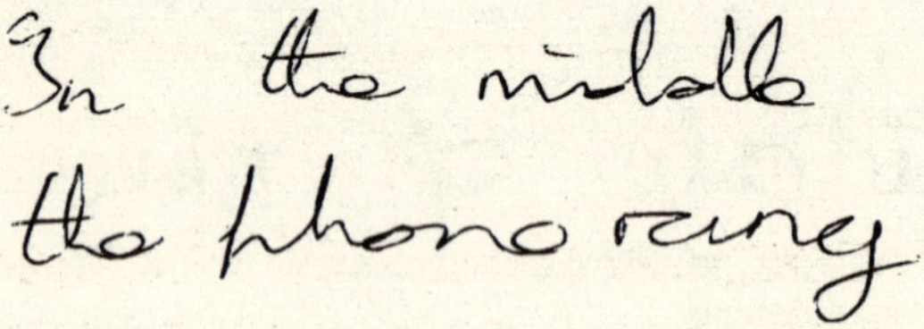

▶ James, in his twenties, could not write fast enough to pass exams

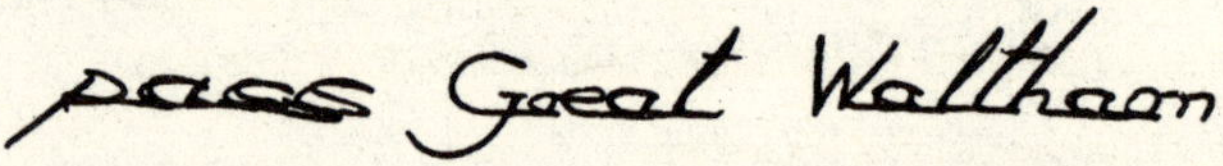

It is obvious at first glance that he had a major movement problem.

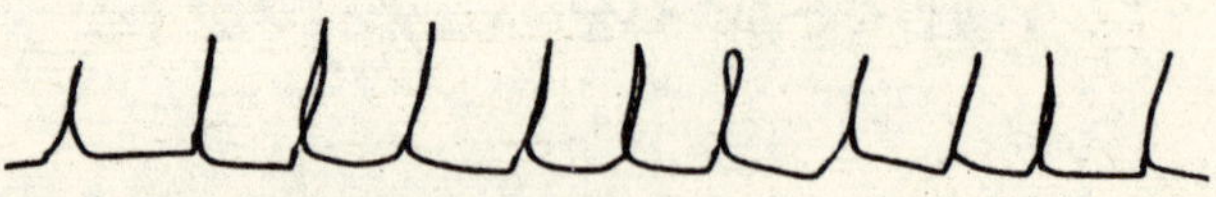

He could not make a curved pattern. In fact, he found it difficult to see the difference between a curved join and a flat one.

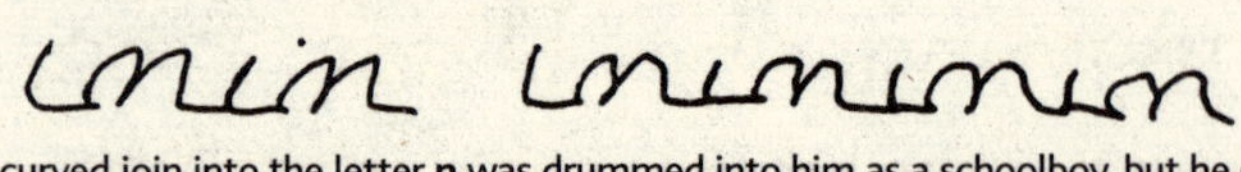

The curved join into the letter **n** was drummed into him as a schoolboy, but he could not learn to make a soft exit stroke out of the letter **i**. He is used to his writing and it does not look strange to him. But his main problem is in perception of form. Luckily, he could see the difference between a zig-zag pattern and his own shapes.

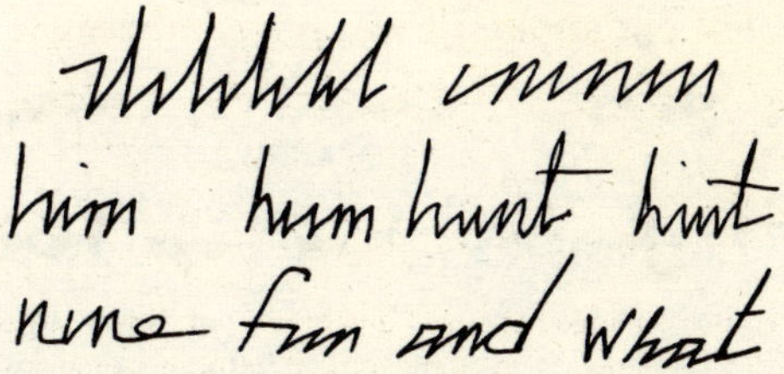

With a zig-zag line it was easy for him to see how simple letters join. At that stage he used triangular letterforms, such as the ***a***.

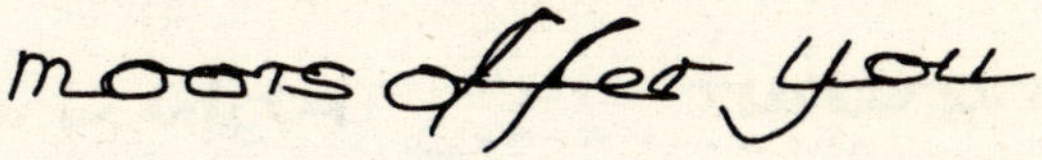

Complicated letters were a great trouble, even going on from an **o** to another letter.

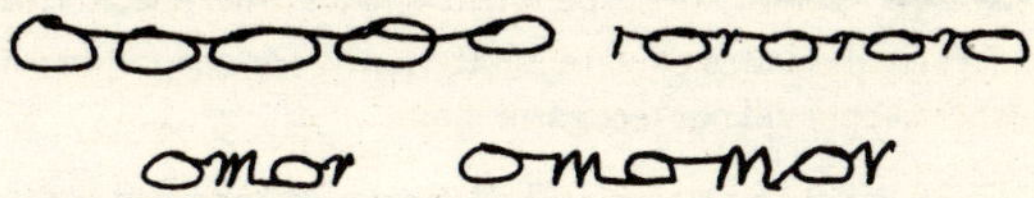

Imagine his predicament: every time he tried to write a new word, there was a new problem.

After a lot of trouble he perceived a simple way of joining the letters of the word 'room' along the top. When he had understood, making the line itself was easy.

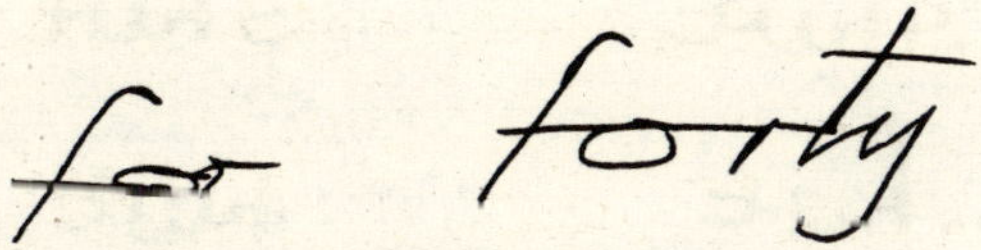

The word 'for' took a lot of untangling.

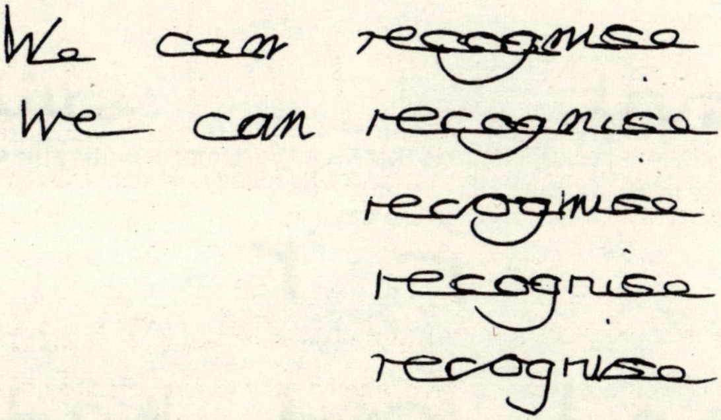

This final sample shows how far he could go in one sitting. He sorted out easily words like 'we' and 'can'. But 'recognise' was still too much.

Matthew left out strokes; it was very confusing

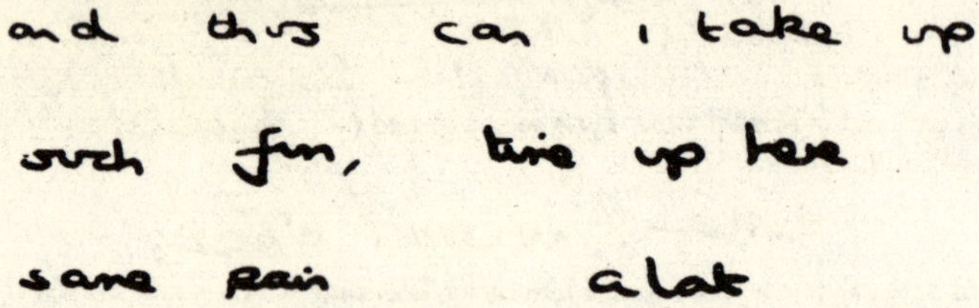

These words read 'and thus can I take up ... such fun ... time up here ... same pain ... a lot'.

Matthew had a very poor idea of correct letterforms. His adaptations made sense to him but other people did not recognize them.

He left out the essential first stroke of the letters **n**, **m** and **r** and the last stroke of the **bb**. They were baffling when they were joined up.

He had no difficulty writing the letters correctly in remedial exercises.

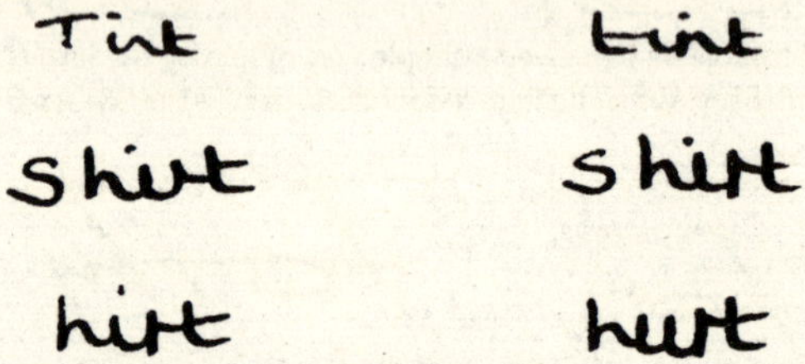

It was more of a problem to persuade him that only with conventional letterforms would other people understand what he had written. The left column still looked correct to him.

Eventually he was persuaded to see that his first attempt at writing the word 'suit' looked more like 'sink'.

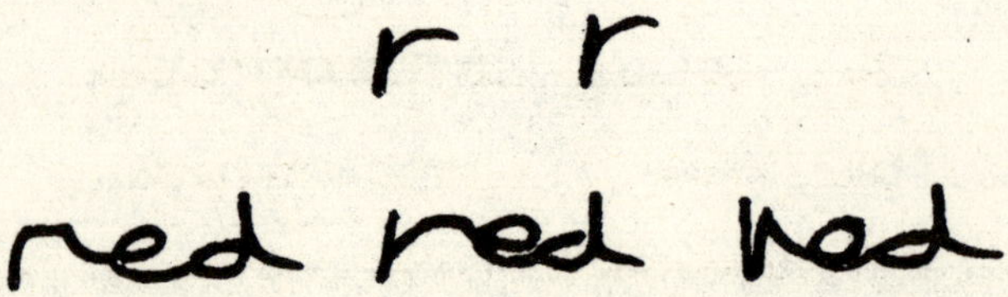

He had no trouble constructing the letter **r**. But he did not know how to join it.

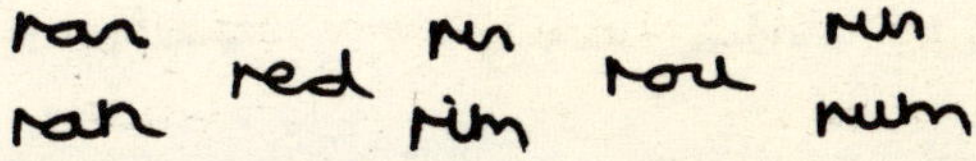

He went through an exercise of joining the letter **r** to each vowel in turn. His **r** went well, but in words where he came across two problem letters he usually did not get both right the first time.

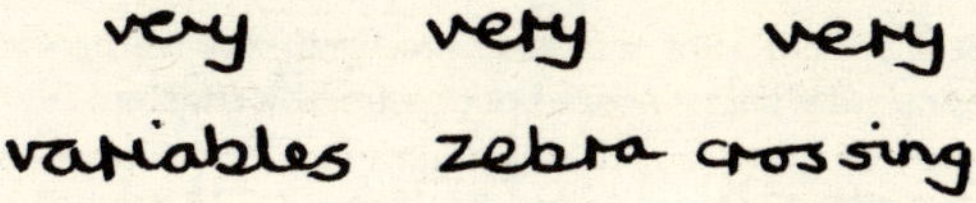

After a very short time he was writing long words.

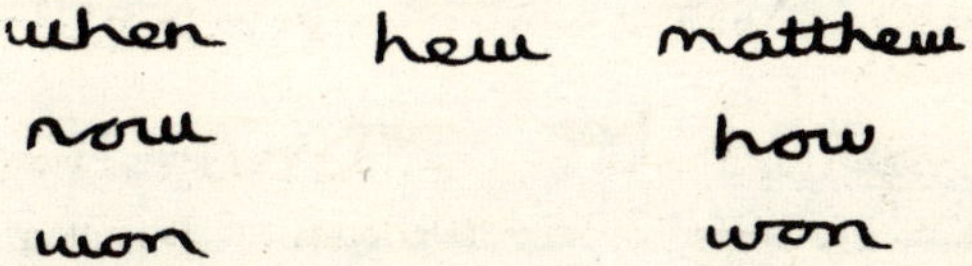

There were still other snags. He made the letter **w** with an exit stroke at the bottom, rather than at the top where it belongs. He was quite ready to change his letterform, but his old way of writing still looked right to him.

Matthew only needed to understand why his letters had to change. At the end of the afternoon, all his letters were correctly constructed. With all the writing he has to do at, the rest will follow naturally.

A couple of weeks later Matthew wrote an interesting and useful letter.

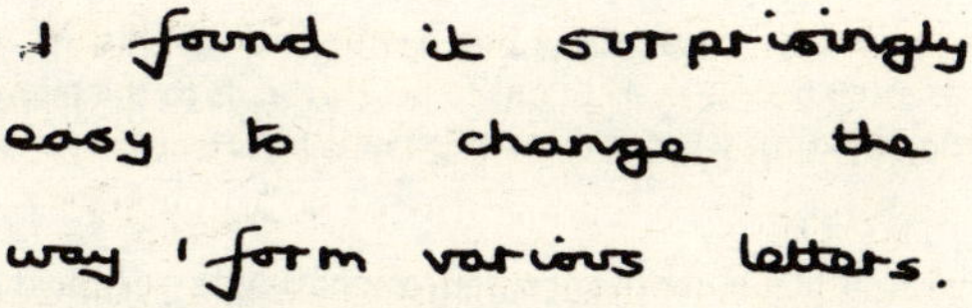

It explained what he felt about his improvement.

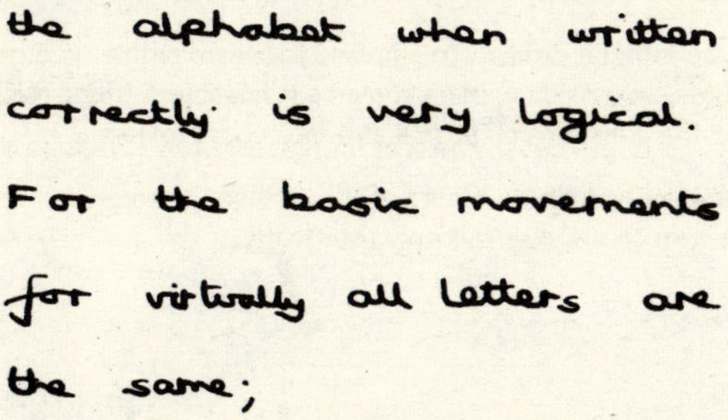

Not only was his writing more legible, with correctly formed letters, but it moved much more smoothly. The only letter that he had not changed was his **u**.

feel the way I actually write some of my letters is now much more flowing

This is a most important point. It should be recognized by teachers and parents. Constructive analytical help is needed, not destructive criticism.

Secondly it is vital that the writer has confidence in his/her own script. Too much criticism leads to a 'seizing up' of the hand; cramped movements and in my case an ever declining script;

Matthew goes on to say: 'I still believe that a writer believes his/her script not to be as bad as other people make it out to be. This leads to the point where you yourself do not know what your writing faults are. Hence, how can one self-correct?'

He felt that, with sufficient motivation, self-diagnosis was 'very possible'. The writer needs to be made aware of possible problems and have a movement model to compare and copy from.

However, if you found it difficult to pinpoint your own problems, even with the diagnostic guide, an outside opinion could be invaluable. A friend might find it easier to read the questions on page 4 and spot your problem.

Sometimes understanding the nature of the problem is more trouble than curing it. Matthew's own case shows this only too clearly.

▶ John's problem was that he wrote too fast

He had a very quick brain and found that, if he slowed his writing down too much, he lost his train of thought. So only a fairly minor adjustment was needed to strike a balance between speed and legibility.

He had been writing with a ballpoint. This allowed him to cut too many corners, and he was writing really too fast to be legible.

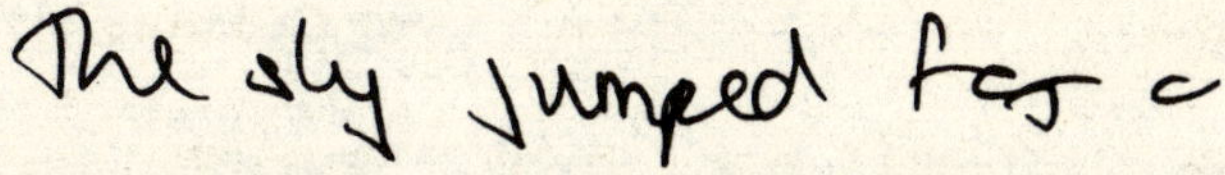

A fibre tip fattened up his writing, which was an advantage, but it still did not slow him down quite enough. So then he experimented with fountain pens.

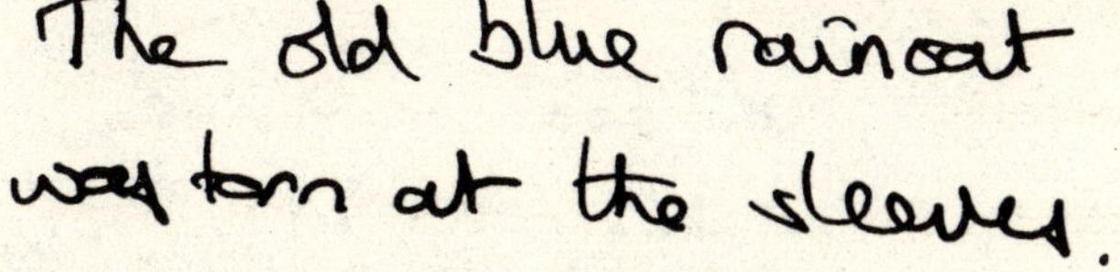

A pen with an ordinary nib made a distinct improvement.

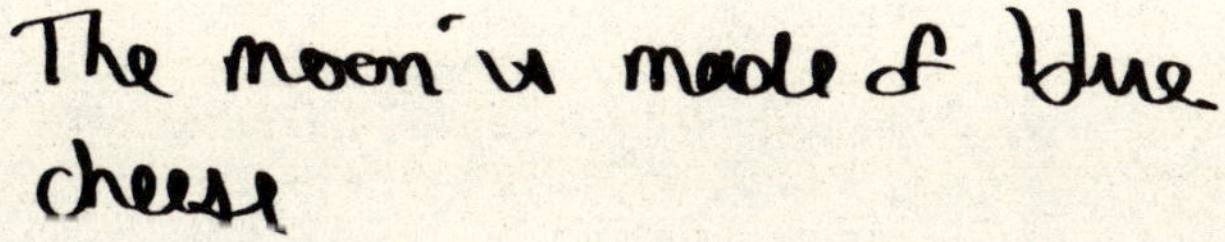

The italic nib disciplined him even more, without slowing him down too much. However, it was a cheap pen with poor ink flow. He set off to search for a better quality italic pen which should help him even further.

Part four

Finishing touches

▶ Margins are important

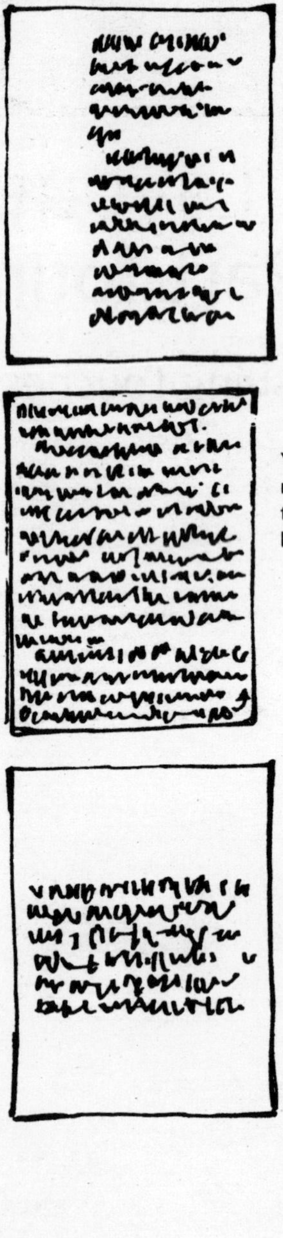

You need some white space on your page. It does not matter much where on the page you put the text. But do not fill the sheet from top to bottom and from side to side.

12

Layout

When you write a letter, does it make the best possible impression? Even if your writing is very good, you are only halfway there.

It matters very much where the writing goes on a page. If you arrange the text carefully, you can make it much easier to read. Your handwriting has many possibilities for expression.

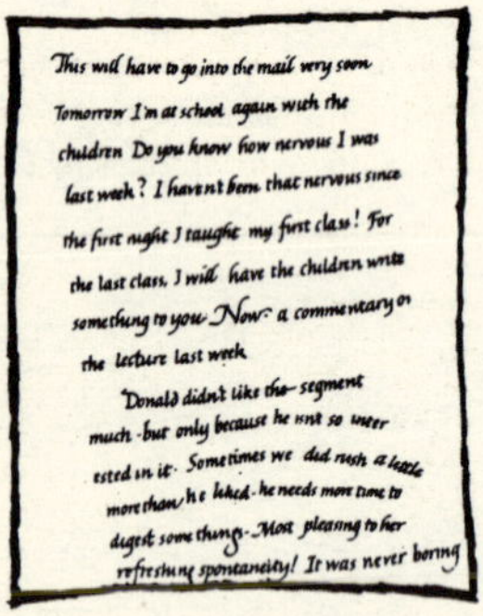

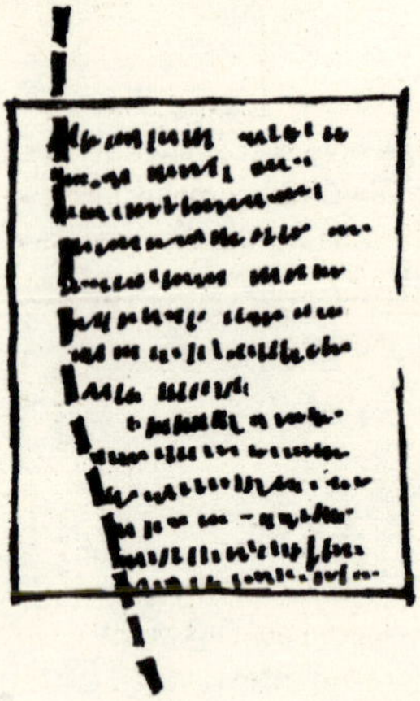

An uneven margin looks very untidy. If you begin half an inch from the edge of the paper you must keep to the same measurement all the way down. A pencilled guideline may help you get used to it.

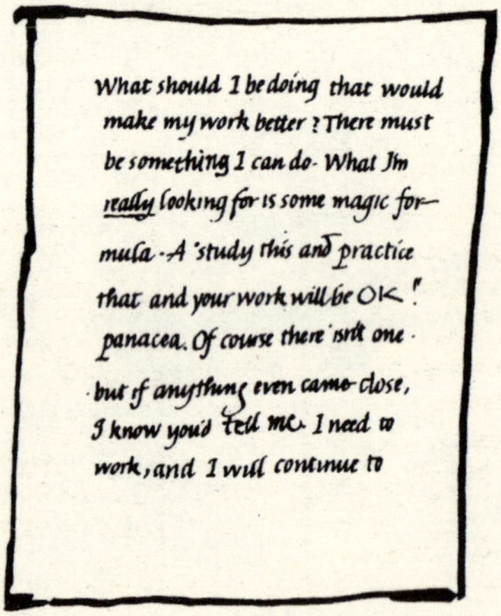

Good word spacing.

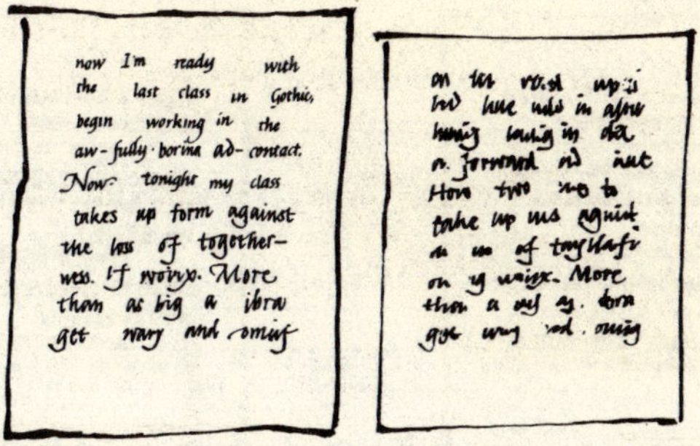

Large word spaces are eyesores. If a wide space in one line is above another in the next line, they combine into a vertical blob of white in the text. A page of writing with wide word spaces can have rivulets of white running down the sheet. It is very ugly.

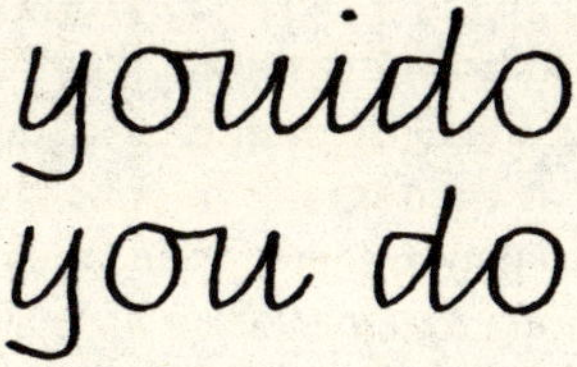

The space between words should be that of an imaginary i with a joining stroke before and after it.

You can give the written word a tone of voice. If you want to add importance to a word, you can underline it. Or you can write it in CAPITALS. (With parentheses you can whisper to your reader.) You can use dashes – as long as you do it in moderation – for a casual aside, and exclamation marks for emphasis, if you handle them with care!!

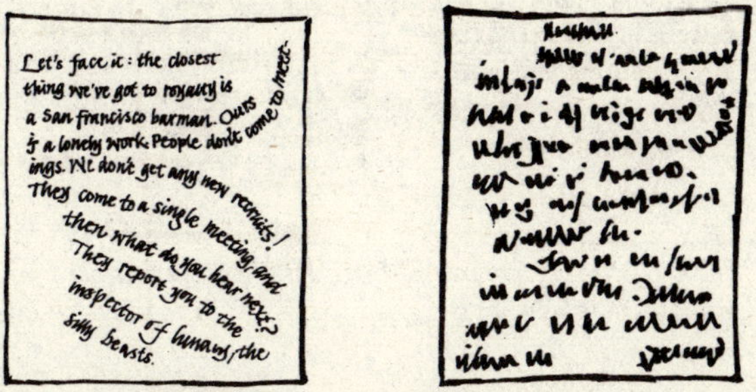

A messy page of text makes many people think that the writer has a messy mind. These examples certainly have their faults: uncertain margins, reluctance to break words between lines and too small a bottom margin.

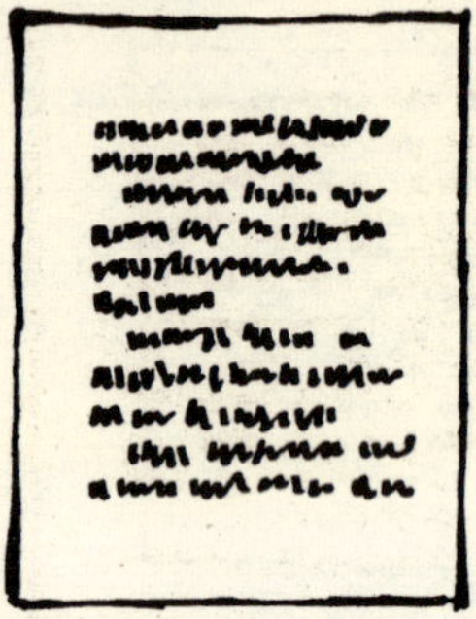

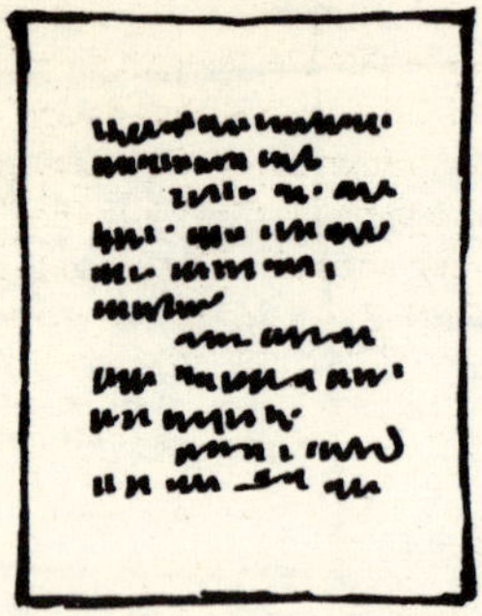

How much do you indent? The page on the left has smaller indentations than the one on the right. Both are quite all right. But you must make up your own mind about what suits you, and keep to it.

Long stretches of text can be tiresome. You can make them easier to read if you divide them into paragraphs. You can indent the first line of a paragraph to your taste. Some people leave a 5 cm (2 inch) gap. Others never indent at all. A few paragraphs that belong together often have a heading of their own: there are many ways that you can fit it to the text.

A letter has many standard parts. Your address goes at the very top. Then you have a small gap. Below that you might put the date and/or the name and address of the person you are writing to. Then there is another gap. Before you start on what you have to say, you will usually have a line of greeting ('Dear . . .'). Then comes the main text. And after that you leave a gap. You say goodbye. Another gap, and you sign your name legibly.

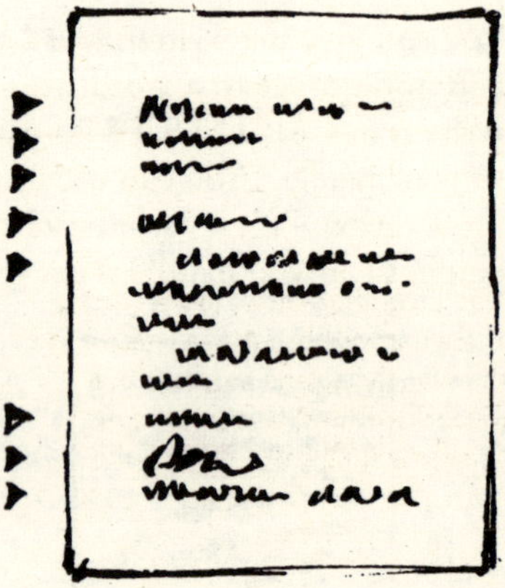

This is the same letter with different ways of presenting it on the page. This first illustration shows tight line spacing. The subheading is fitted into the first paragraph and underlined. It suits rather large writing.

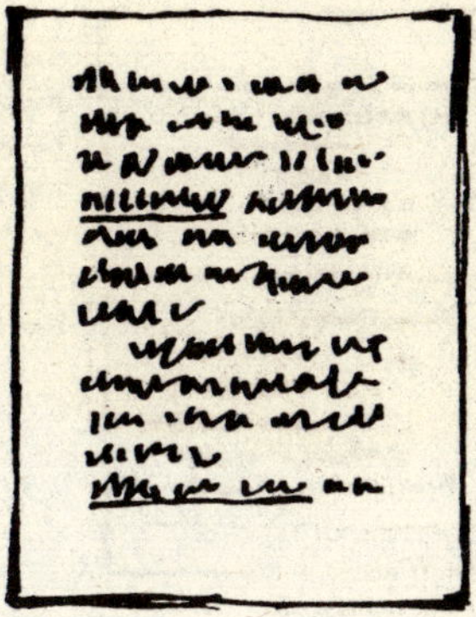

This illustration shows a somewhat looser spacing. There is a gap above the subheading. It has a line to itself and therefore does not need underlining. Note that you usually indent every paragraph to show that a new one is beginning. But after a subheading it is obvious and you do not need to indent.

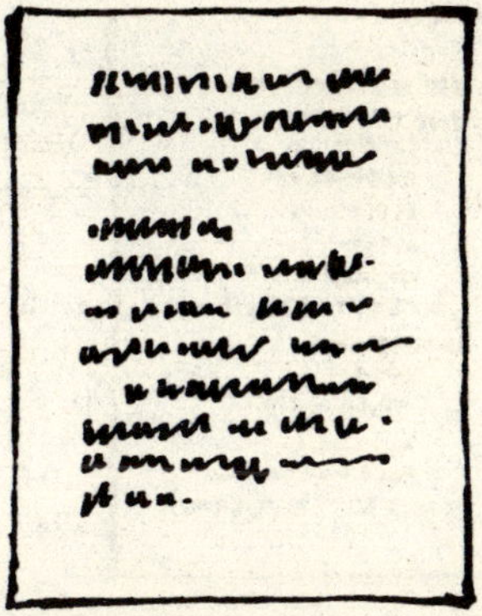

This Illustration shows loose spacing. There is a wide gap (three lines) above the subheading and a smaller one (oneor two lines) below. This suits smaller writing best.

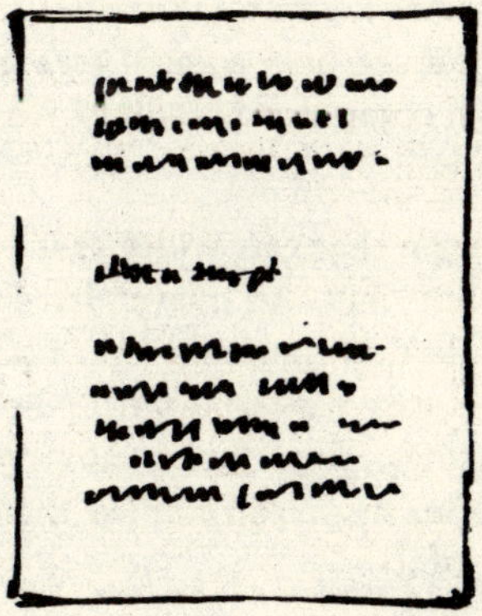

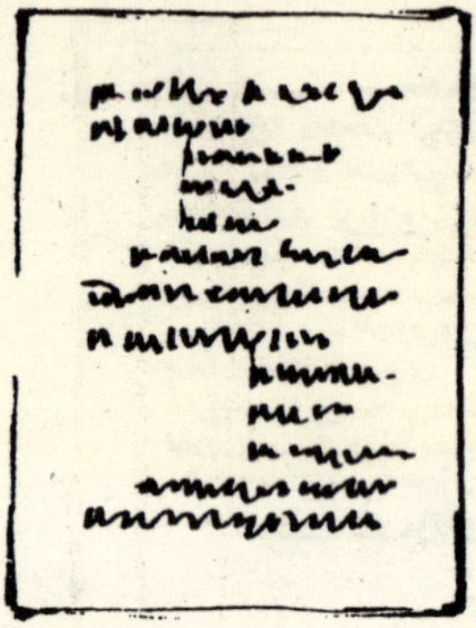

Indented blocks of text (lists, etc.) always pose a problem. Sometimes they have to be balanced on the page by eye. There is a temptation to let the end of the preceding line determine how deep the indentation is and let the list begin where the line ends. This is a bad habit.

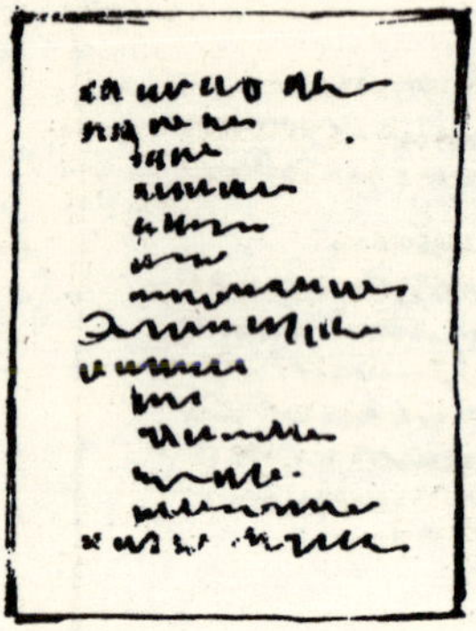

Your indentation should always be the same, whether it is the first line of a paragraph or a whole block of quotation.

Margins are also important. A sheet that is so full of writing that it has no margins at all is uninviting to the eye. Have you ever noticed how a small area of text on a large sheet of paper is almost compulsive reading? Advertisers know this and use it all the time.

A margin that gets wider as it goes down the page is not a pleasant sight. An uneven left-hand margin looks untidy. It should be straight and your right-hand margin reasonably tidy. This is very easy to do. All you need is to draw two vertical guidelines. The left one shows you where to start, the right one where to stop. You can use them for a while, until you get the hang of it.

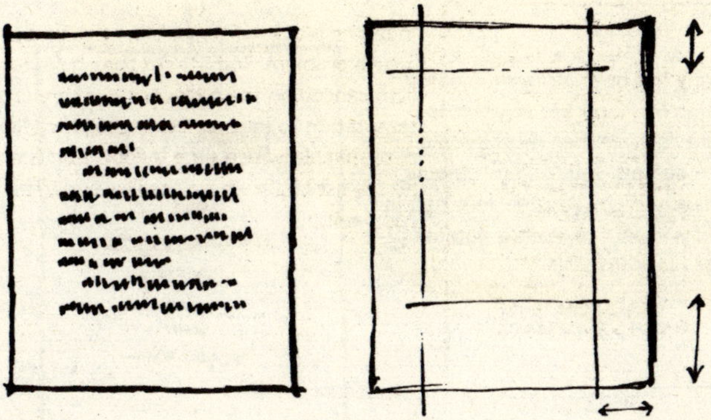

The most popular proportion of margins has a narrow one on top, wider on both sides and a deep bottom margin, up to twice the top one. But there are plenty of other ways which are just as attractive.

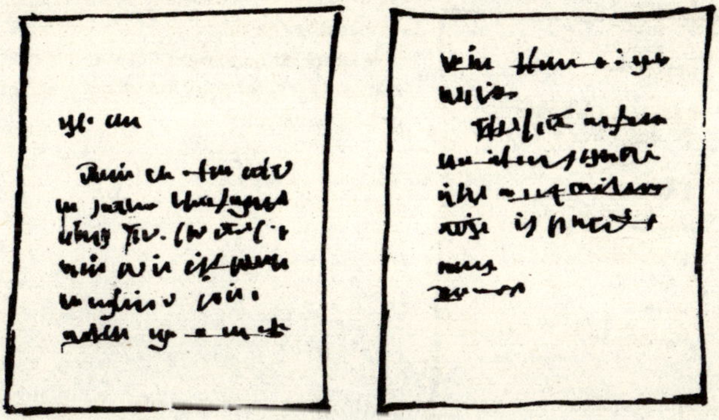

The same amount of text can fit the page in many ways. At the top a letter is fitted snugly on to one page with conventional margins. Below, the same text with looser spacing fits two pages of the same margin proportions.

It looks much better if you divide a word between lines rather than let it stick into the margin.

How you arrange the words on a sheet depends on what you are writing: class notes are different from a furious letter of complaint. But these are a few general considerations that you might want to keep in mind. Use your text and the white spaces imaginatively. Make a rough draft or two for all important letters.

Centring has been a time-honoured tradition for hundreds of years. It is more difficult than most people realize, and any faults show up only too clearly. If you arrange your text in this way, expect to make a number of careful plans first.

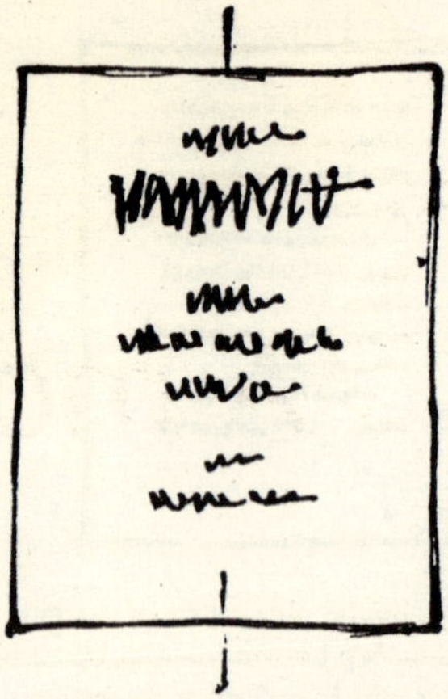

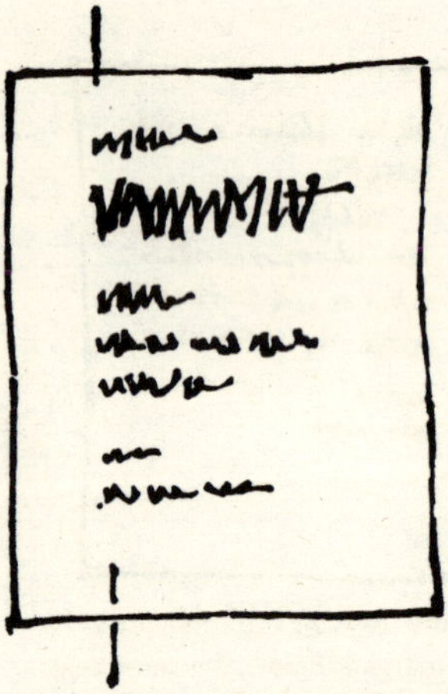

The same text. Lining up to the left margin is usually a safer solution when you can get away with it.

You have now learned a method of writing. It is a series of movements that enables you to write quickly.

Other people must be able to read what you have written and, of course, you must be able to decipher it yourself. You have learned about the basic shapes that your letters must have to be recognizable.

In this chapter you have learned how to make your writing look attractive on the page.

These are the basic elements of writing.

13

A more formal model

What formal writing is, and how to do it

This chapter has a slightly different purpose from the rest of the book, in that it teaches you a formal hand to use on special occasions. The letters of this model are the same as those in the teaching alphabet in Chapter 8. The difference is that they are written with a broad-edge nib. First learn the model. When you have mastered it, you can do as you did with the training alphabet and modify it so that you can write it more freely. But the thicks and thins will still be there to give their special character to your hand.

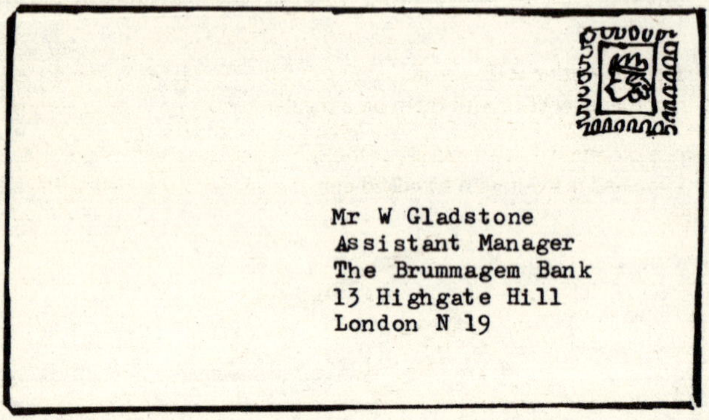

If your bank manager gets two envelopes likes these, which of them do you think he will open first?

Formal handwriting catches people's attention.

Formal writing is different from your everyday writing in two main ways. One is that the pen you use is probably not of the kind you normally write with. The other is that you want a formal hand to do something quite different from just carrying the words of a message. You are also drawing beautiful letters in order to please the eye.

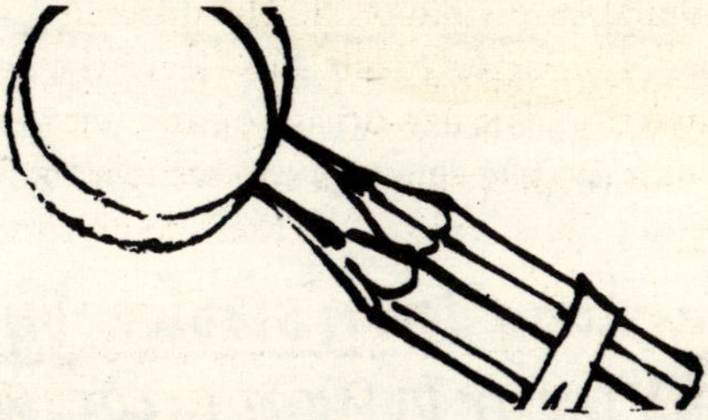

The principle of writing with a broad-edge pen. (You are not supposed to strap pencils together and write with them on a regular basis!)

If you make a circle with two pencils at the same time, you get two overlapping circles. If you had made it with an edged pen, the gap would of course have been full of ink.

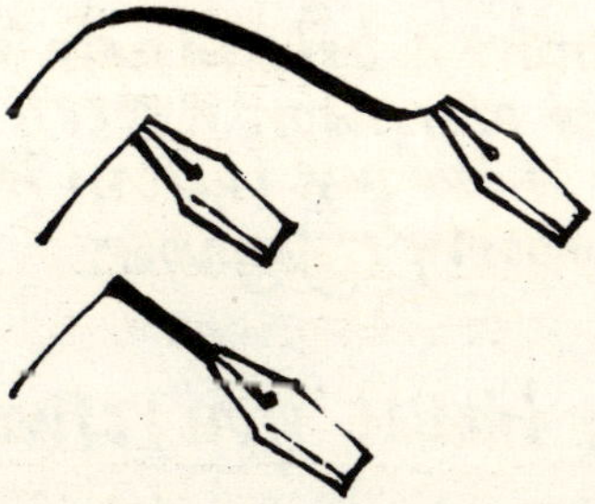

A pen with a thin but broad edge makes thick and thin lines by the angle that the edge has to the stroke it is writing. A sideways line along the edge gives you a thin line. A stroke in the direction of the pen barrel makes a broad line. A wavy line has thicks and thins according to the angle of the edge to the line.

You can write a formal hand with all kinds of pens. But the kind you are going to learn about here is the broad-edge pen. Broad-edge pen is a loose term. It can be a special kind of fibre tip with a point that looks like the business end of a chisel. It can be a wing feather that has one end cut to a writing point. Most people use a fountain pen with a special nib.

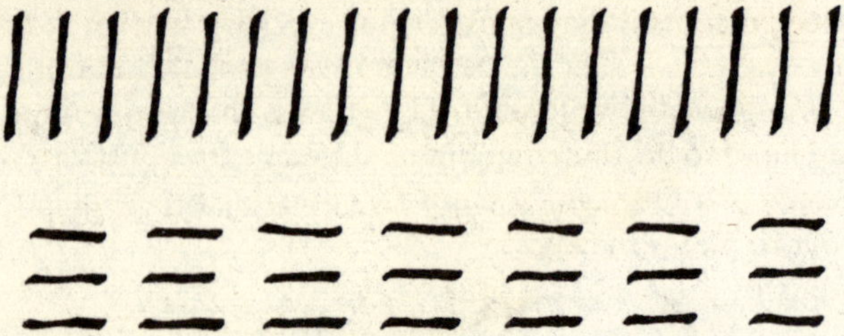

The best exercises to teach your hand to control a broad-edge pen are downstrokes, side by side, and horizontal lines in a brick-wall pattern. Write a page or two of each. Take your time. You can pick up speed once you have mastered the pen.

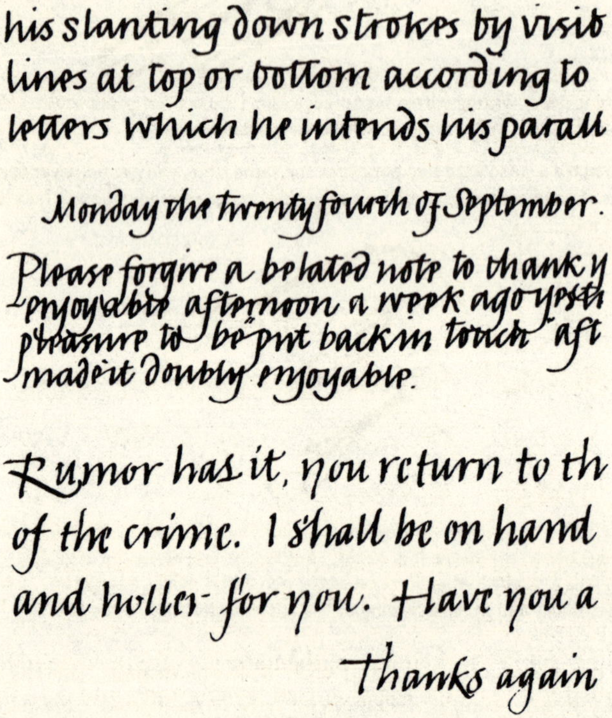

Three samples of flowing, regular italic handwriting. The first two are the work of the same writer, first as a student, then several years later.

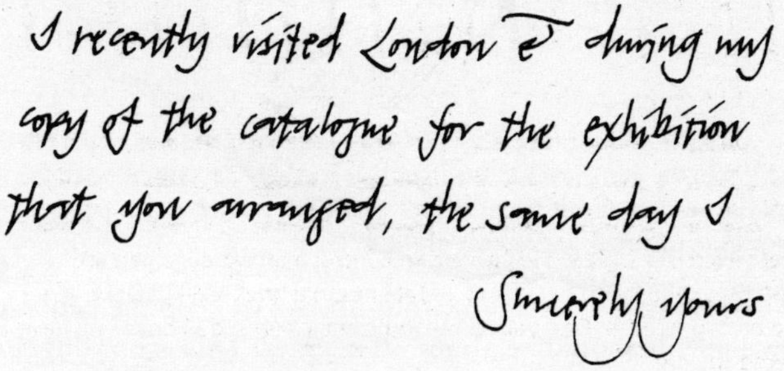

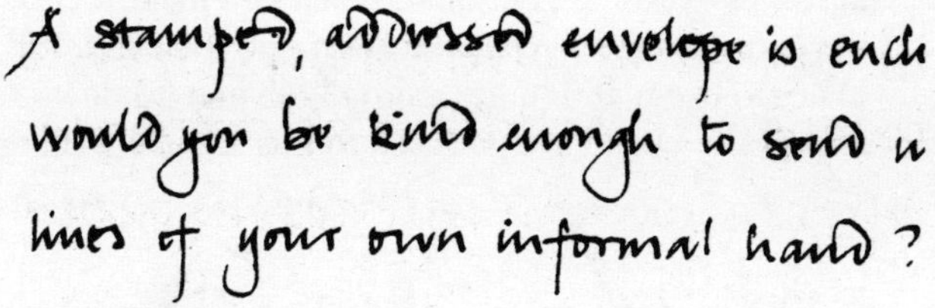

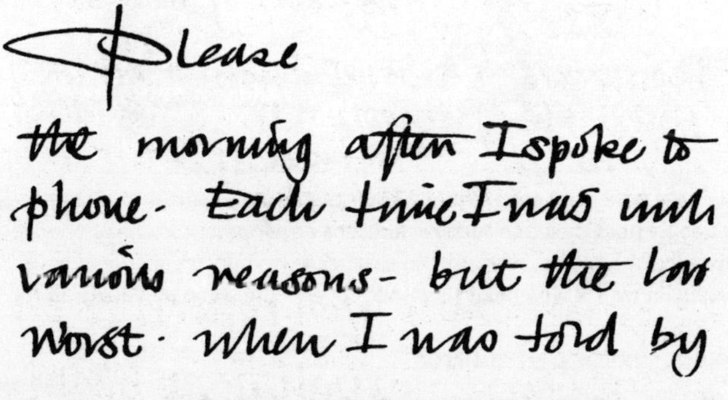

When you write with a broad-edge pen, the direction of your stroke makes it thick or thin. The shape that the pen makes is very logical. When you make a curve with a broad-edge nib, the swelling can be worked out mathematically. You can see that even better if you tape together two pencils and write with them as if they were a pen (see page 167).

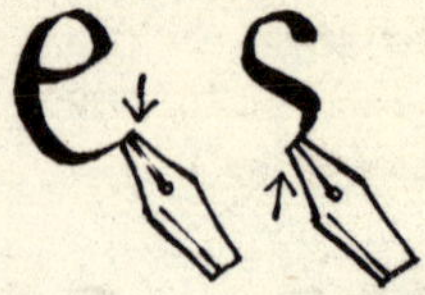

When you write with a broad-edge pen, concentrate on the side of the nib that is ahead. When the pen moves to the right you probably pay attention to the right side of the nib. But do not forget to look at the left side when the pen goes to the left, as in the tricky movement of the letter s.

The first thing you should learn is always to keep the pen at the same angle. It should be about 30 degrees. This is not difficult at all. If you feel like turning your hand when you make a curve, look at the patterns below. That will soon put you right. It is usually easier to begin with quite a broad nib and go down to a narrower one when you have got used to this style of writing.

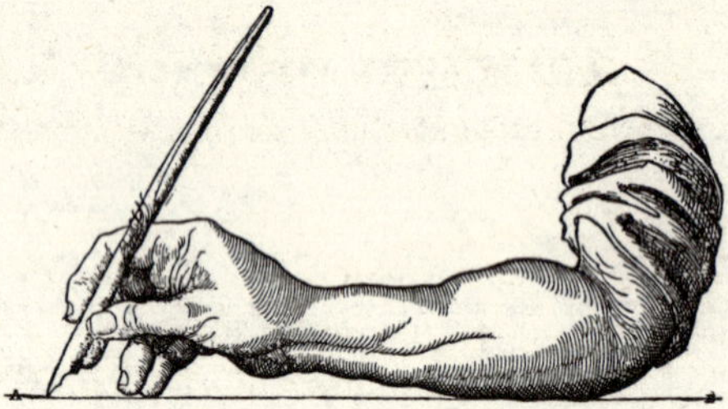

People have held their pens in many kinds of grip. As a matter of fact, the way most people hold their pen today is a recent development in the history of handwriting. A hundred years ago no teacher in his right mind would have allowed it. However, you must keep more or less the same pen angle all the time.

Exercises for pen control

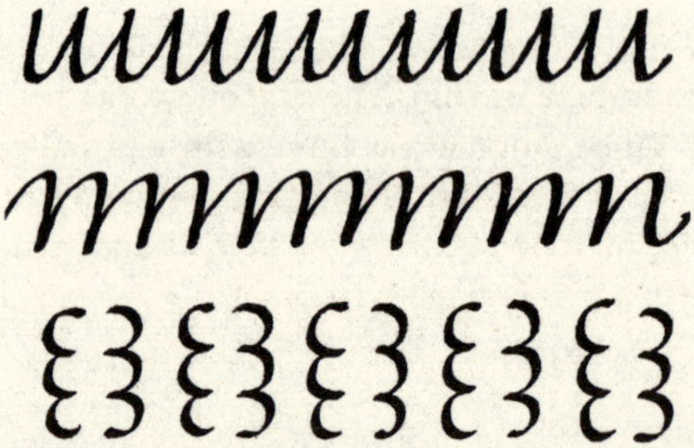

These lines should be written out separately. Aim at a machine-like regularity in the downstrokes. This matters more when you write with a broad-edge pen than when you write with a ballpoint.

You must also remember to let the pen write with the entire edge of the nib. Otherwise you lose the thick-and-thin effect that the pen gives your writing.

abc abc

A correct pen angle is essential when you use an edged nib. The example on the left shows the correct angle. On the right an incorrect angle has caused bad writing, even if the letterforms are the same. Here the thicks and thins have got into the wrong places.

When you have learned to keep a constant angle, you can play with the letterforms by altering the angle a bit. The letter **N** can look better when you write it at a steeper angle and the **Z** often improves if the edge of the pen is almost flat on the baseline.

ZZ NN

The small letters should all be written with a constant pen angle. Not so with the capitals.

When you make letter shapes with a broad-edge pen, you should pay attention to one side as your eyes follow the nib. If the pen is moving to the left, you concentrate on the left side. If it is going to the right, it is the right side of the nib that matters. This is particularly important when you are joining one stroke to another.

abcdefgh
ijklmno
pqrstu
vwxyz

Consistent pen angle is most important, even if you do not use exactly the angle shown in the model. It is less important with the capitals than the small letters. You can safely experiment with small variations of pen angle, even within the same letter, such as **A**, **M** and **W**.

abcdefgh

ijklmno

pqrstu

vwxyz

It is easy to write the small letters with a broad-edge pen. You follow the same method as you did when you wrote them before. Begin all your exercises slowly and only allow your hand to write faster when you have got used to the movements.

abcdefgh

ijklmno

pqrstu

vwxyz

Use the model alphabet until you have a feel for the letters. Do not allow your own handwriting to modify the characters until you know them well. Keep your pen angle constant.

When should you use a formal hand?

You cannot write a formal hand as fast as an informal one. When you are writing under the usual pressures, there is little point in attempting beautifully measured strokes. They slow you down too much.

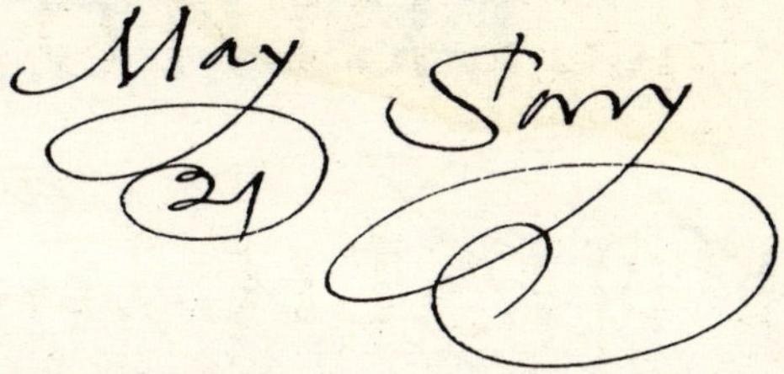

Some beautifully free flourishes.

CAPITALS ARE MORE DIFFICULT TO WRITE THAN SMALL LETTERS

Some of the characters do not get the very best proportion between thicks and thins unless you alter the pen angle. The letter **N** needs less slant and the **Z** more slant than the others.

ABCDEFG

HIJK

LMNOPQ

RSTUVW

XYZ

Even if the letters seem to be of the same height, they are not. If you are writing a word in capitals, you have to make the letters uneven in height so they all look the same.

A letter with a flat top such as an **E** looks taller than an **A** or an **O**. Remember to let curves or corners go a little bit outside the straight lines.

SLAVE SLAVE

Badly spaced capitals look even worse than badly spaced small letters. A common error is to fit them as closely together as possible. The general **area** between letters should be the same, as on the left.

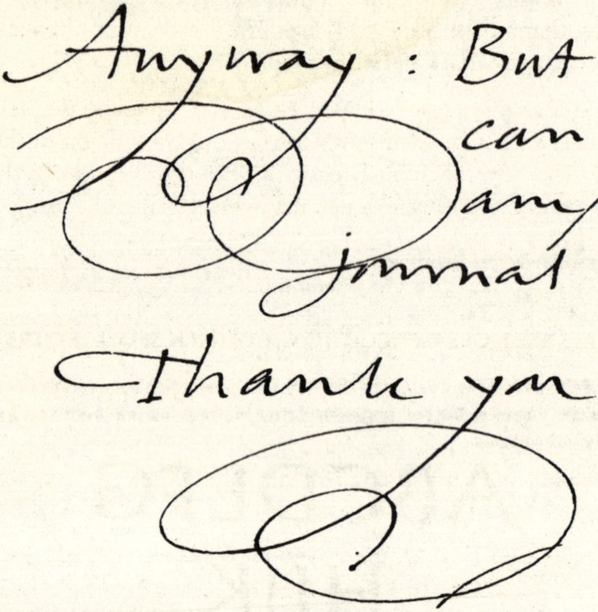

More flourishes and some beautiful capital letters too.

Epilogue

This books asks the reader to do a lot of hard work. Handwriting is so much the product of our habits, our very natures, that a deliberate, sustained effort is needed to make any lasting change. That can be agony.

Important changes can be produced by techniques so simple that many will curse themselves for not having thought of them before. They are ridiculously easy, like having the paper in the right position or choosing a pen that you actually like using.

Some changes are more difficult to make. By a careful process of self-testing the reader has been led to discover some of the personal habits causing the handwriting difficulties that need to be overcome; and, with some delicacy, has been invited to reflect on their possible underlying causes. The reader will then have exercised the opposing qualities needed to make any change permanent and real: for tension, to practise relaxing; for impatience, to practise self-control; for slowness, to practise moving without anxiety or hesitation.

Although no part of the purpose of this book, it may be an incidental advantage that those who have faithfully followed the exercises will discover that at least some of the qualities they have been acquiring in their handwriting stay with them in other activities too.

But above all, this book is discreet. None but the reader will ever really know...

John Sassoon